American Psychiatric Press, Inc.

1400 K STREET, N.W.
WASHINGTON, D.C. 20005

DIAGNOSIS AND TREATMENT OF ANXIETY DISORDERS

DIAGNOSIS AND TREATMENT OF ANXIETY DISORDERS

Edited by
Robert O. Pasnau, M.D.

Note: The editor and the contributors worked to ensure that all the information in this book concerning drug dosages, schedules, and routes of administration is accurate at the time of publication and consistent with standards set by the U.S. Food and Drug Administration and the general medical community. As medical research and practice advance, however, therapeutic standards may change. For this reason and because human and mechanical errors sometimes occur, we recommend that readers follow the advice of a physician directly involved in their care or the care of a member of their family.

Library of Congress Cataloging in Publication Data
Main entry under title:

Diagnosis and treatment of anxiety disorders.

Includes index.
1. Anxiety—Addresses, essays, lectures.
   I. Pasnau, Robert O.
(DNLM: 1. Anxiety disorders—Diagnosis
2. Anxiety disorder—Therapy. WM 172 D536)
RC531.D53   1984   616.85'223   84-447
ISBN 0-88048-022-X

Printed in the U.S.A.

This book is dedicated to Janet.

Contents

Preface

Most of my professional life has been spent in consultation liaison psychiatry and psychosomatic medicine, and I have seen many patients in consultation every day. The most frequent, almost ubiquitous, clinical symptom I have encountered is anxiety. Every psychiatrist who treats patients, whatever his or her field of practice, encounters anxiety. We confront it not only in our patients, but also in ourselves. Eugene Pumpian-Mindlin taught me that when a psychiatrist treats an anxious patient, it is probably better that one of the two people in the room *not* be anxious, preferably the psychiatrist. I know that he would agree that the lack of information about the biology, epidemiology, and treatment of anxiety and anxiety disorders has left much about which the clinician ought to be "anxious."

Recent developments in psychopharmacology have emphasized the heterogeneous quality of anxiety. Current clinical case studies have revealed that there are important subgroups among anxiety sufferers, and the result is that a more rational and selective choice of treatment modalities is now available. Yet despite these early promises, much confusion remains in both diagnosis and treatment. The epidemiology of the anxiety disorders is in a very rudimentary stage as well.

There is no question about the upsurge of interest in anxiety and anxiety disorders. In planning a symposium sponsored by the UCLA Department of Psychiatry and Behavioral Sciences that was held in Los Angeles in 1982, we anticipated that a maximum of 150 psychiatrists would be interested in attending a full Saturday's meeting devoted to examining the subject. Instead, 300 available openings were reserved within the first two weeks following the announcement, and we turned away hundreds of psychiatrists by mail and telephone. The symposia on the anxiety disorders held at 1982 and 1983 spring meetings of the American Psychiatric Association were attended by more than 2,000 psychiatrists at these combined meetings. These are indications of the great professional interest in obtaining current information about this burgeoning area of psychiatric practice.

The goal of this volume is to present the current thinking and research on the psychobiology, psychodynamics, psychophysiology, and psychotherapy of these disorders. It is not meant to be an exhaustive treatise on research in anxiety; it is intended to be a practical volume for the clinician and student for rapid review of the subject. The carefully selected references found at the end of each chapter are provided for those who are interested in pursuing a more in-depth study.

Following my brief history and review of the anxiety disorders is a chapter by Herbert Weiner on the Psychobiology of Anxiety and Fear, a chapter by Kenneth I. Shine on Anxiety and Physical Illness, and a chapter by Louis Jolyon West and Kerry Coburn on Posttraumatic Anxiety. The second part of the book covers the treatment of the anxiety disorders. A chapter on The Psychodynamic View of Anxiety by John C. Nemiah is followed by David Sheehan's chapter on Strategies for Diagnosis and Treatment of Anxiety Disorders, and Richard L. Heinrich's chapter on Behavioral Approaches to the Evaluation and Treatment of Anxiety Disorders. The concluding chapter is on the relationship between Anxiety and Sleep by Robert L. Williams and Ismet Karacan.

The editor is grateful to the above contributors for their cooperation in meeting deadlines for a timely production, to the editors of American Psychiatric Press, Inc., for their encouragement of the project and willingness to speed the production following submission of the manuscript, and to Mrs. Naomi Rosenberg and Ms. Jennifer Benjoya for their help in the typing and production of the manuscripts and art work. I would also like to express my appreciation for the major contribution of Arlene Goldberg in her painstaking and dedicated work as Consulting Editor.

Robert O. Pasnau, M.D.
Los Angeles, California
March, 1984

The Authors

Kerry Coburn, Ph.D.
Staff Research Associate
Department of Psychiatry and Biobehavioral Sciences
UCLA Neuropsychiatric Institute
Los Angeles, California

Richard L. Heinrich, M.D.
Adjunct Assistant Professor of Psychiatry
Department of Psychiatry
UCLA School of Medicine
Chief, Behavioral Rehabilitation Research
Sepulveda Veterans Administration Medical Center
Sepulveda, California

Ismet Karacan, M.D. (Med) D.Sc.
Professor of Psychiatry and
Director of Sleep Disorders Clinic
Baylor College of Medicine
Associate Chief of Staff for Research
Veterans Administration Hospital
Houston, Texas

John C. Nemiah, M.D.
Professor of Psychiatry
Harvard Medical School
Psychiatrist-in-Chief
Beth Israel Hospital
Boston, Massachusetts

Robert O. Pasnau, M.D.
Professor of Psychiatry
Department of Psychiatry and Biobehavioral Sciences
UCLA School of Medicine
Director of Adult Psychiatry
UCLA Neuropsychiatric Institute
Los Angeles, California

David Sheehan, M.D.
Assistant Professor of Psychiatry
Harvard Medical School
Director of Anxiety Research
Massachusetts General Hospital
Boston, Massachusetts

Kenneth I. Shine, M.D.
Professor and Executive Chairman
Department of Medicine
UCLA School of Medicine
Los Angeles, California

Herbert Weiner, M.D.
Professor of Psychiatry
Department of Psychiatry and Biobehavioral Sciences
UCLA School of Medicine
Chief of Behavioral Medicine
UCLA Neuropsychiatric Institute
Los Angeles, California

Louis Jolyon West, M.D.
Professor and Chairman
Department of Psychiatry and Biobehavioral Sciences
UCLA School of Medicine
Director, UCLA Neuropsychiatric Institute
Los Angeles, California

Robert L. Williams, M.D.
Professor of Psychiatry
D.C. and Irene Ellwood Professor and Chairman,
Department of Psychiatry
Baylor College of Medicine
Houston, Texas

1

The Anxiety Disorders

Robert O. Pasnau, M.D.

The Anxiety Disorders

Robert O. Pasnau, M.D.

Introduction

Severe anxiety disorders disrupt the lives of millions of Americans. Some victims of these disorders suffer from irrational fears of situations and objects from reptiles or rodents to riding on elevators. Others experience sudden panic attacks that are marked by feelings of impending doom and intense fear. Some may experience a persistent anxiety that lasts for months. Still others suffer anxiety following a psychologically traumatic event, such as a serious accident, military combat, incarceration, rape, or other violence.

Almost everyone feels anxious from time to time, sometimes with understandable reasons. However, some people experience feelings of anxiety that come to dominate their lives. In extreme cases, individuals may wash their hands 50 or more times a day to remove unexplained germs. Others, who are considered to be victims of agoraphobia, may refuse to leave the safety of their homes for many years. Still others, suffering from undiagnosed anxiety disorders, may suffer intractable insomnia that disturbs their sleep and affects the quality of their lives. This insomnia may be the result of a maladaptive coping mechanism for some individuals who are unable to deal with the stressful events in their lives.

Psychiatrists have been diagnosing and treating anxiety disorders since before the time of Freud. But often diagnostic descriptions for anxiety disorders are vague, the causes for them are unknown or disputed, and treatments are only moderately effective. Psychotherapeutic approaches in which the therapist attempts to help patients understand the underlying causes of anxiety and then to overcome it, although varying widely in effectiveness, are effective in treating simple phobias and chronic and moderate anxiety states. The most prevalent form of treatment is psychopharmacology. Tranquilizers, which are routinely prescribed to ease anxiety, are the most widely used drugs in medical practice today; however, recent research indicates that antidepressant medications may be more effective than tranquilizers in treating phobias and obsessive-compulsive disorders. Mechanisms by which these drugs achieve their effect are still not known.

Although anxiety disorders are widespread and frequently are not diagnosed by our medical colleagues, research on the anxiety disorders is only now beginning to evolve. The National Institute of Mental Health (NIMH) is spending $3 million a year on anxiety research. Although this is a modest investment compared with $19 million on schizophrenia and $15 million on depression, research into treatment strategies, diagnosis, and genetic susceptibility to anxiety is progressing rapidly. All of these research findings are increasingly useful in current psychiatric practice.

According to a recent household survey reported by NIMH, 8 percent of the adult population of the United States have symptoms that could be diagnosed as anxiety disorder and another 11 percent suffer from serious anxiety symptoms that are related to physical illness. Thus it appears that one-fifth of the adult population—some 30 million people in all—exhibit symptoms of significant anxiety. Yet there is no reliable epidemiologic data about these disorders, and according to the Chief of Psychopathology and Clinical Methods Section of NIMH, research in this area of psychiatry is "in a quagmire" (1). Many mental health professionals believe that the incidence, prevalence, and severity of these disorders are seriously underestimated.

Genetic and Familial Aspects of Anxiety

For many years it was suspected that anxiety disorders were familial diseases. Beard found that neurasthenia was largely a hereditary disorder (2); DaCosta's description of the "irritable heart" in 1871 was the first of many names given to panic disorder (3); and a family history of nervous disorder was found in almost half of the World War I soldiers who were diagnosed as having DaCosta's Syndrome (4). Cohen and others found that two-thirds of their patients with neurocirculatory asthenia had a family history of the same disorder (5), and Noyes and his colleagues noted an 18 percent correlation of anxiety neurosis in first-degree relatives. In these studies (which may well have underestimated the incidence and prevalence) twice as many females were affected by this disorder as males (6).

In the early 1960s, Klein and Fink found that individuals with panic attacks were suffering from a distinct form of an anxiety disorder that should be separated from the other forms of anxiety. It was shown that patients with these attacks had experienced severe episodes of separation anxiety in childhood and that these attacks were frequently precipitated by the loss of an important person in their lives. They proposed that panic anxiety had a close biological relationship to separation anxiety. Perhaps more importantly, they demonstrated that the pharmacological treatment of panic disorder differs from that of the generalized anxiety disorder (7).

More recently, Crowe and others found a likely genetic component in panic disorders. There appeared to be a very small correlation between panic disorder and generalized anxiety disorder in family members (8). In 1982, Raskin and her co-workers found that patients with both panic disorders as well as generalized anxiety had a similar incidence of early separation, separation anxiety in childhood, and separation as a precipitant of symptoms. However, the groups differed significantly in that those with panic anxiety had a higher incidence of grossly disturbed childhood environments and major depressive episodes. The results of Raskin and others' study support the validity of the distinction between categories of generalized anxiety and panic anxiety (9).

Developmental and familial factors may be very important in diagnosis of anxiety disorders, and a careful family history should be taken in each case. Although the absence of anxiety disorder in a patient's family cannot rule out the presence of an anxiety disorder, the finding of the disorder in a family member should raise a high level of suspicion about the ultimate nature of the patient's problem. The family history of a depressive disorder does not rule out the diagnosis of anxiety because many patients with anxiety disorders have first-degree relatives with primary affective disorder (10).

During the past few years, it has been proposed that many patients with panic disorder may have mitral valve prolapse syndrome (Barlow's syndrome), which can produce symptoms associated with panic attacks. The data are inconclusive, however, in part because of the sophisticated diagnostic techniques that are required to diagnose the disorder. Crowe and others also found that family morbidity risk for panic disorder is very high, but that it is independent of a diagnosis of mitral valve prolapse syndrome (8). Hartman and others, in their study of 141 patients with mitral valve prolapse, found that the prevalence of panic disorder in the group was 16 percent, a figure slightly higher than in ordinary cardiologic patients. However, they caution that this high prevalence may be due to a selection bias in favor of highly symptomatic individuals (11). Other studies tend to be inconclusive (12). It is important that patients with panic disorder be evaluated for mitral valve prolapse because of the high risk they run for developing subacute bacterial endocarditis following minor surgical procedures.

Anxiety states can also occur sometimes as a prodromal

phase of an acute depressive illness (13). Because these patients respond remarkably well to treatment with mono-amine oxidase inhibitors, this response to a drug which is not essentially an anxiolytic agent indicates the need to take into account the close relationship that may exist between the anxiety states and affective disorders. Considerable overlap in the symptoms of anxiety states and depression does exist. At the UCLA Affective Disorder Clinic, anxiety was found to be present in more than 80 percent of the patients suffering from a depressive illness or diagnosed as having an affective disorder. Many of these patients present to the clinic with a self-diagnosis of anxiety disorder, but with the characteristic vegetative signs of depression.

Taxonomic Evolution

Psychodynamic Contributions

Prior to the adoption of the first edition of the *Diagnostic and Statistical Manual of Mental Disorders* (DSM-I) in 1952 (14), a rather simple, psychoanalytically oriented diagnostic schema was generally accepted by most practicing psychiatrists. In this taxonomy two anxiety disorders were described: anxiety neurosis and anxiety hysteria (15).

Anxiety neurosis was considered to be the simplest expression of a neurotic disorder. In this situation the conflict was not disguised, displaced, or symbolized. It was described as personality disequilibrium per se. If the illness was characterized by a sudden onset, it was termed "panic anxiety" or "panic attack." Many of these patients were observed to be incapacitated by the "fear of fear." This was described as a fear secondary to the uncertainty of never knowing when a panic attack would occur.

Following DaCosta's description of "irritable heart," (3) the disorder carried many names including "soldier's heart," "neurocirculatory asthenia," "cardiac neurosis." The attacks were characterized by shortness of breath, palpitations, chest pains, smothering sensations, dizziness, unreality, paresthesia, hot and cold flashes, sweating, faintness, trembling or shaking, and the fear of dying. When the disorder had a gradual onset it was usually termed "free-floating anxiety." Free-floating anxiety was often known to be accompanied by somatic symptoms as well. The chronic anxiety state usually was called neurasthenia. This condition often progressed over a period of years to a state characterized by weakness, disability, regression, and secondary depression (2).

Anxiety hysteria was defined as one of the simplest methods of neurotic adaptation. By utilizing the defense mechanisms of projection and fixation, the conflict was felt to be circumscribed and the defense was strengthened. The patient's behavior became dominated by the need to avoid contact with the feared object. Over the years, the phobias acquired an "apparent life of their own." It was noted that phobic patients often became more and more generalized in their fears, progressing from relatively simple phobic states to profound states of agoraphobia (fear of open spaces) and/or claustrophobia (fear of closed spaces).

In this diagnostic formulation, defense against anxiety was presumed to be at the heart of every neurosis (16). An example of this was the obsessive-compulsive neurosis, which was marked by the process of converting the anxiety into repetitive behavioral or cognitive symptoms in an elaborate or regressive way. But this neurosis was usually considered to be separate from the anxiety neurosis.

DSM-I

The first *Diagnostic and Statistical Manual of Mental Disorders*, published by the American Psychiatric Association in 1952, accepted this basic nomenclature, but in keeping with its traditional Meyerian approach, adopted the terminology of "reaction" (14). Thus, anxiety *neurosis* became anxiety *reaction*; anxiety *hysteria* became phobic *reaction*.

Many psychiatrists who are now in practice and who had their residency training during the 1950s and 1960s continue to be influenced by these earlier diagnostic and psychodynamic formulations. As Rosenbaum has pointed out, anxiety reaction was the routine diagnosis used for the anxious patient, and the prescription of sedative hypnotic agents served as the major treatment (17). Similarly, phobic reaction was the routine diagnosis for phobic patients, and insight-oriented psychotherapy aimed at deriving the unconscious source of the conflict was the treatment of choice.

DSM-I made an important contribution to the United States and world psychiatry. It was reprinted 20 times through 1967 and distributed widely around the world. DSM-I was also used in the United States for statistical coding of psychiatric case records. No other country had provided itself with an equivalent official manual of improved diagnostic terms.

DSM-II

A decade and a half after the publication of DSM-I, DSM-II was adopted in 1968 (18). DSM-II was an attempt to reflect the growth of the concept that U.S. psychiatrists were not alone in the world, and that there was a need to standardize diagnoses across international borders. It was also believed that the rapid integration of psychiatry with the rest of medicine was enhanced by DSM-II, using terminology and classifications closely integrated with those of other medical specialties. The scholars and practitioners who developed DSM-II returned to the pre-DSM taxonomy to collaborate more closely with the developers of the International Classification of Diseases (ICD-8), which was approved by the World Health Organization in 1966 to become effective in 1968. Thus, DSM-II accomplished two important tasks by promoting international psychiatric research and a closer integration of psychiatry with medicine.

In terms of the evolution of the concept of the anxiety disorders, DSM-II avoided terms which carried with them implications regarding either the nature of the disorder or its causes, but was explicit about causal assumptions when they were integral to a diagnostic concept. DSM-II relied heavily on the concept of neurosis. Noting that anxiety was the chief characteristic of the neurosis, it is observed that anxiety could be felt and expressed directly and controlled unconsciously and automatically by conversion, displacement, and various other psychological mechanisms. In contrast to the psychoses, the neuroses were defined as manifesting neither gross misinterpretation nor distortion of external reality nor gross personality disorganization. No matter how severely handicapped by their symptoms, neurotics were not classified as psychotic "because they are aware that their mental functioning is disturbed" (18).

DSM-II described ten neuroses: anxiety neurosis (anxiety reaction in DSM-I), hysterical neurosis (both conversion and dissociative type), phobic neurosis (phobic reaction in DSM-I), obsessive-compulsive neurosis, depressive neurosis, neurasthenic neurosis (psychophysiologic nervous system reaction in DSM-I), depersonalization neurosis, hypochondriacal neurosis, and other neurosis. Anxiety neurosis was characterized by anxious overconcern extending to panic and frequently was associated with somatic symptoms. Phobic neurosis was characterized by intense fear of an object or situation that the patient consciously recognized as no real danger. However, DSM-II retained the concept "that phobias are generally attributed to fears *displaced* to the phobic object or situation from some other object of which the patient is unaware."

DSM-III

Twelve years after the publication of DSM-II, the third edition of the *Diagnostic and Statistical Manual of Mental Disorders* was published in 1980 (19). This publication had a stormy birth, with hundreds of field tests, contributions from teams of scientists and practitioners, and many changes from within the American Psychiatric Association's Assembly and Board of Trustees. DSM-III represents a genuine departure from the older taxonomy, although through compromise and negotiation, some of the terms (particularly neurosis) are retained in parentheses. The major underlying unifying concept is that of psychiatric disorder. What was termed a "reaction" in DSM-I and a "neurosis or psychosis" in DSM-II, becomes a "disorder" in DSM-III. The anxiety disorders are classified in two major categories: phobic disorders and anxiety states. In introducing the anxiety disorders, anxiety is noted either as the predominant disturbance or as experienced if the individual attempts to master the symptoms. DSM-III also contributes to the taxonomic evolution by excluding the diagnosis if it was due to another disorder such as schizophrenia, an affective disorder, or an organic mental disorder. It is estimated that from 2 to 4 percent of the general population has at some time had a disorder which would be classified as an anxiety disorder, and that each of these disorders is more common among family members of individuals who have anxiety disorders than in the general population.

Phobic disorders are defined as having the essential feature of persistent and irrational fear of a specific object, activity, or situation that results in a compelling desire to avoid the dreaded object, activity, or situation. The fear is recognized by the individual as unreasonable or excessive in proportion to the actual dangerousness presented. Three forms of phobic disorders are described in DSM-III: (a) agoraphobia, (b) social phobia, and (c) simple phobia.

Agoraphobia is defined as a marked fear of being alone or being in public places from which escape might be difficult or help not available in case of sudden incapacitation. Normal activities increasingly are constricted as the fears or avoidance behavior dominate the individual's life. The most common situations avoided involve being in crowds, such as on a busy street or in crowded stores; or being in tunnels, on elevators, on public transportation, or on bridges. Often these patients insist that a friend or family member accompany them whenever they leave their home (Table 1-1).

Table 1-1.   DSM-III Diagnostic Criteria for Agoraphobia

A. Marked fear thus avoidance of:
  • being alone
  • public places where escape is difficult or help not available
B. Significant life disruption
C. Phobia not due to other disorders

Source: American Psychiatric Association, 1980.

Social phobia is described as a persistent irrational fear of and compelling desire to avoid situations in which the patient may be exposed to the scrutiny of others. There is also a fear that the individual may behave in a manner that will be humiliating or embarrassing. Marked anticipatory anxiety occurs if the individual is confronted with the necessity of entering into such a situation and therefore the patient attempts to avoid it. This disorder is a significant source of distress and is recognized by the patient as excessive and unreasonable. Examples of social phobias are fears of performing or speaking in public, eating in public, writing in the presence of others, or using public lavatories. Considerable generalized anxiety may also be present in patients suffering from social phobia (Table 1-2).

Table 1-2.   DSM-III Diagnostic Criteria for Social Phobia

A. Persistent irrational fear/avoidance of:
  • situations where scrutiny is possible
  • acting in a humiliating/embarrassing manner
B. Significant distress due to recognition of irrationality of fear
C. Phobia not due to other disorders

Source: American Psychiatric Association, 1980.

Simple phobia is defined as a persistent, irrational fear of and compelling desire to avoid an object or situation other than being alone in a public place away from home (agoraphobia) or of humiliation or embarrassment in certain social situations (social phobia). This category represents a residual category of phobic disorder. The disorder is a significant source of distress and the patient recognizes that the fear is unreasonable or excessive. The most common simple phobias involve animals such as mice, insects, snakes, or cats; fear of closed spaces (claustrophobia); or fear of heights (acrophobia) (Table 1-3).

Table 1-3.   DSM-III Diagnostic Criteria for Simple Phobia

A. Persistent irrational fear/avoidance of:
  • object
  • situation
  other than Agoraphobia or Social Phobia situations
B. Significant distress due to recognition of irrationality of fear
C. Phobia not due to other disorders

Source: American Psychiatric Association, 1980.

Anxiety states are divided by DSM-III into four basic categories: (a) panic disorder, (b) generalized anxiety disorder, (c) obsessive-compulsive disorder, and (d) posttraumatic stress disorder (PTSD). Although anxiety states topped the list of neuroses in DSM-II, and in the psychoanalytic formulation represented the purest form of psychiatric disturbance, they are listed in second place in DSM-III.

Panic disorder is defined as recurrent anxiety attacks (panic) that occur unpredictably. Certain situations, however, including driving a car, may become associated with panic attack. The panic attacks are manifested by sudden onset of intense apprehension, fear, or terror, often associated with feelings of impending doom. The most common symptoms experienced during an attack are shortness of breath (dypsnea), chest pain or discomfort, palpitations, choking or smothering sensations, dizziness, vertigo, unsteady feelings, feelings of depersonalization or derealization, parasthesias, hot and cold flashes, sweating, fainting, trembling, shaking, and fear of dying, going crazy, or doing something uncontrolled during the attack. The attacks usually last minutes; more rarely they last hours. The patient often develops varying degrees of nervousness and apprehension between the attacks (Table 1-4).

Table 1-4. DSM-III Diagnostic Criteria for Panic Disorder

A. At least 3 panic attacks in 3 weeks occurring in the absence of:
 • physical exertion
 • a life-threatening situation
 • organic illness
 • phobic stimulus

B. Attacks manifested by sudden intense fear/apprehension + 4 or more symptoms:
 • fear of dying/losing control
 • dyspnea • faintness • palpitations
 • chest pain/discomfort • sweating
 • choking/smothering sensation • shaking
 • feelings of unreality • paresthesias
 • hot/cold flashes • dizziness/vertigo

C. Not due to physical disorder or other mental disorders

D. The disorder is not associated with agoraphobia

Source: American Psychiatric Association, 1980.

Generalized anxiety disorder is characterized by a persistent generalized anxiety of at least one month's duration, but without the specific symptoms that characterize phobic disorders, panic disorders, or obsessive-compulsive disorders. The diagnosis is *not* made if the disturbance is due to other physical or mental disorders such as hyperthyroidism or depression. Although the specific manifestations of anxiety vary from individual to individual, generally there are signs of motor tension, autonomic hyperactivity, apprehensive expectations, and vigilance and scanning. Mild depressive symptoms are commonly associated with this disorder (Table 1-5).

Table 1-5. DSM-III Diagnostic Criteria for Generalized Anxiety Disorder

A. Symptoms from 3 of 4 categories:
  • Motor tension
  • Autonomic hyperactivity
  • Apprehensive expectation
  • Vigilance and scanning
B. Anxious mood continuous (at least 1 mo.)
C. Not due to other disorder
D. At least 18 years of age

Source: American Psychiatric Association, 1980.

Obsessive-compulsive disorder is defined as recurrent obsessions or compulsions. Obsessions are defined as persistent ideas, thoughts, images, or impulses that are not experienced as voluntarily produced, but rather as thoughts that invade the patient's consciousness and are experienced as repugnant or senseless. Attempts are made to ignore or suppress them, which may lead to anxiety or depression. Compulsions are defined as repetitive and seemingly purposeful behaviors that are performed according to certain rules in a stereotyped fashion. The behavior is not an end in itself, but is designed to produce or prevent some future events or situations. However, the activity is not connected in a realistic way with what it is designed to produce or prevent, and may be clearly excessive. Attempts to suppress or ignore the compulsions frequently lead to anxiety or depression (Table 1-6).

Table 1-6. DSM-III Diagnostic Criteria for
Obsessive-Compulsive Disorder

A. Either obsessions or compulsions
B. Significant source of distress or significant life disruption
C. Not due to other disorders

Source: American Psychiatric Association, 1980.

Posttraumatic stress disorder is defined as the development of characteristic symptoms following a psychologically traumatic event that is generally outside the range of usual human experience. The characteristic symptoms involve reexperiencing the traumatic event, a numbing of responsiveness to or reduced involvement with the external world, and a variety of autonomic dysphoric or cognitive symptoms. Symptoms of depression and anxiety are common, and in some instances may be sufficiently severe to be diagnosed as an anxiety or depressive disorder. Patients may experience hyperalertness, sleep disturbance, guilt, and memory impairment. They tend to avoid activities that arouse the recollection of the event, because symptoms are intensified by events resembling the original trauma (Table 1-7).

Table 1-7. DSM-III Diagnostic Criteria for
Posttraumatic Stress Disorder

A. Existence of recognizable stressor
B. Reexperiencing the trauma by:
  • recurrent recollections and/or
  • recurrent dreams and/or
  • sudden acting/feeling as if event is reoccurring
C. "Psychic numbing"
D. At least 2 of the following symptoms:
  • hyperalertness
  • sleep disturbance
  • guilt
  • memory impairment
  • avoid activities that arouse event recall
  • symptom intensification by events resembling traumatic event

Source: American Psychiatric Association, 1980.

Differential Diagnosis of Anxiety Disorders

When diagnosing patients with anxiety disorders, three major considerations exist: (a) Is the patient suffering from a physical or medical disease? (b) Is the patient suffering from another psychiatric disorder, especially depression or schizophrenia? and (c) Is the patient suffering from alcohol or substance abuse disorder?

Differentiating Anxiety Disorders from Physical Diseases

Because physical symptoms are so dominant in anxiety disorders, a thorough medical differential is required when diagnosing anxiety. Respiratory and cardiovascular symptoms that accompany any medical condition associated with sympathetic arousal can be confused with anxiety disorders. These include such conditions as congestive heart failure, myocardial infarction, pulmonary embolus, and anaphylaxis. In the case of recurrent attacks, differential diagnosis of tachyarrhythmia, such as paroxysmal atrial tachycardia (PAT), is difficult. However, the sinus tachycardia from a panic attack will rarely exceed a pulse of 140 per minute, whereas PAT is usually faster. PAT may be associated with an EKG abnormality such as the Wolfe-Parkinson-White syndrome. PAT is unlikely to respond to reassurance or anxiolytic therapy.

The vestibular diseases, or labyrinthitis, for example, can cause the same type of dizziness that one sees with anxiety. It is a relatively common disorder. Menopause may cause some of the peripheral vasomotor symptoms that accompany anxiety. In addition, over-the-counter decongestant preparations, some of which may contain sympathomimetic agents, can produce cardiovascular effects similar to those caused by anxiety.

Catecholamine-secreting tumors such as pheochromocytoma, while quite rare, should also be considered. Other diagnostic possibilities include blood loss, temporal lobe epilepsy, hypoglycemia, serum electrolyte imbalance, serum calcium abnormalities, and mitral valve prolapse syndrome (Table 1-8).

Table 1-8. Medical Differential Diagnosis of Panic Disorder

Congestive heart failure	Blood loss
Myocardial infarction	Temporal lobe epilepsy
Pulmonary embolus	Hypoglycemia
Anaphylaxis	Electrolyte, calcium, and other metabolic disorders
Tachyarrhyrthmia (e.g., paroxysmal atrial tachycardia)	Drug abuse
Hyperthyroidism	Drug withdrawal
Pheochromocytoma	Mitral valve prolapse (Barlow's syndrome)

Source: Rosenbaum JF, 1981. Reprinted with permission.

It must be remembered that anxiety may play a role in any organic illness, and in that context, it usually responds well to reassurance and appropriate tranquilizers. Chapter 3 of this volume covers this subject more fully.

Hall and others studied 650 patients referred for psychiatric treatment and found that 10 percent of them had primary medical conditions responsible for the psychiatric symptomatology. The third most common psychiatric diagnosis given to these medically ill patients was anxiety. Included in the differential diagnoses were such conditions as caffeinism, hypocalcemia, hypoglycemia, thyroid disorder, and the side effects from other medications as well as those previously mentioned (20). The psychiatrist should not be misled by reports that the internist or family practitioner has failed to find an organic condition or that organic conditions have been excluded. Medical diagnosis is not an infallible science, and many organic disorders may be misdiagnosed or overlooked by medical colleagues.

Differentiating Anxiety Disorders from Other Psychiatric Disorders

A major difficulty in diagnosing anxiety disorders is that anxiety can occur as a symptom in most psychiatric disorders. A proper psychiatric history is sometimes difficult to obtain, however. For example, in the early stages of schizophrenic disorder, patients may be very frightened when symptoms first appear and refuse to talk about hallucinatory voices or blocking of thinking. Careful mental status examination is essential in these cases.

Perhaps the most important distinction to be made is between anxiety and depressive illnesses. Patients with depression are likely to have a family history of depression, and there may have been previous depressive episodes. The characteristic psychomotor and vegetative signs of depression usually are not present in the anxiety disorders, however. These signs include loss of appetite, loss of weight, loss of energy, and loss of libido. Many patients present with a combination of anxiety and depression. There are anxious patients who are depressed, and there are depressed patients who are anxious. Rickels has found that 70 percent of all neurotic-depressed patients have significant anxiety (21).

Alcohol, Substance Abuse, and Anxiety

For years, individuals have self-medicated for the treatment of anxiety and depression. In biblical times, King Saul was reported to have used alcohol to treat his anxiety and depression. One needs only to travel on a modern jet aircraft to observe the number of individuals who overuse alcohol in an attempt to control the anxiety associated with travel and flying. Probably all anxious patients have used either alcohol or some other legal or illegal substance. The fact that diazepam is the most widely prescribed drug in the world indicates the degree to which physicians are placing reliance on substances that have a high potential for abuse.

Most alcohol users tend to have a significant amount of either anxiety or depression or both. Sometimes it is difficult to determine whether the primary disorder is a substance abuse disorder, or whether the correct disorder is anxiety disorder with symptomatic alcoholism. Although the distinction may be difficult to make, the history of the present illness is not complete without an evaluation of the use of alcohol and other substances (22).

The Psychiatric Rating Scale

Quantifying the degree of symptomatology is useful both to patients and for tracking the symptomatic progress of the course of treatment. It is also very useful in evaluating the degree of anxiety in a particular patient for research or therapeutic purposes.

In 1959, Hamilton designed a psychiatric rating scale designed to assist in the management of patients and to provide a reliable means of documenting the patient's improvement (23). Using 14 symptoms commonly experienced by anxious patients, the Hamilton Anxiety Rating Scale is designed to be given easily and to help elicit the patient's subjective responses to the degree of anxiety. Most psychiatrists who use this evaluation administer it before the treatment and then repeat it periodically during the course of the therapy, usually at weekly intervals. The 14 items measure both physical and emotional symptoms of anxiety, scaled from mild to grossly disabling. Some psychiatrists find that the scale serves to enhance the doctor/ patient relationship, others find the use of such instruments to be intrusive or trivializing. Nonetheless, the use of such scales can be used practically by primary care physicians as well as psychiatrists to provide a useful guide of patient response from visit to visit (Table 1-9).

Case Studies

The examination of individual cases is helpful in pointing out the complexity and often overlapping problems encountered by the clinician. The first three cases of panic disorder, phobic disorder, and obsessive-compulsive disorder come from the author's clinical practice. The fourth case, that of a delayed posttraumatic stress disorder (PTSD) in a Vietnam veteran was published recently by Wise from the Wilford Hall Medical Center, Lackland Air Force Base, San Antonio, Texas (24).

Panic Disorder

The patient is a 32-year-old entertainer who spent her adolescence studying acting. As a teenager, she was a serious actress but had a very restricted social life. Her mother, a somewhat overwhelming "stage mother," kept

Table 1-9.   Hamilton Anxiety Rating Scale

Item		*Rating*
Anxious mood	Worries, anticipation of the worst, fearful anticipation, irritability	_____
Tension	Feelings of tension, fatigability, startle response, moved to tears easily, trembling, feelings of restlessness, inability to relax	_____
Fears	Of dark, of strangers, of being left alone, of animals, of traffic, of crowds	_____
Insomnia	Difficulty in falling asleep, broken sleep, unsatisfying sleep and fatigue on waking, dreams, nightmares, night terrors	_____
Intellectual (cognitive)	Difficulty in concentration, poor memory	_____
Depressed mood	Loss of interest, lack of pleasure in hobbies, depression, early waking, diurnal swing	_____
Somatic (muscular)	Pains and aches, twitchings, stiffness, myoclonic jerks, grinding of teeth, unsteady voice, increased muscular tone	_____

Instructions: This checklist is to assist the physician or psychiatrist in evaluating each patient as to his degree of anxiety and pathological condition. Please fill in the appropriate rating: None=0 Mild=1 Moderate=2 Severe=3 Severe, grossly disabling=4

Source: Hamilton M, 1959. Reprinted with permission.

Table 1-9. Hamilton Anxiety Rating Scale *(continued)*

Item		Rating
Somatic (sensory)	Tinnitus, blurring of vision, hot and cold flushes, feelings of weakness, picking sensation	———
Cardio-vascular symptoms	Tachycardia, palpitations, pain in chest, throbbing of vessels, fainting feelings, missing beat	———
Respi-ratory symptoms	Pressure or constriction in chest, choking feelings, sighing, dyspnea	———
Gastro-intestinal symptoms	Difficulty in swallowing, wind, abdominal pain, burning sensations, abdominal fullness, nausea, vomiting, borborygmi, looseness of bowels, loss of weight, constipation	———
Genito-urinary symptoms	Frequency of micturition, urgency of micturition, amenorrhea, menorrhagia, development of frigidity, premature ejaculation, loss of libido, impotence	———
Autonomic symptoms	Dry mouth, flushing, pallor, tendency to sweat, giddiness, tension headache, raising of hair	———
Behavior at interview	Fidgeting, restlessness or pacing, tremor of hands, furrowed brow, strained face, sighing or rapid respiration, facial pallor, swallowing, belching, brisk tendon jerks, dilated pupils, exophthalmos	———

Instructions: This checklist is to assist the physician or psychiatrist in evaluating each patient as to his degree of anxiety and pathological condition. Please fill in the appropriate rating: None=0 Mild=1 Moderate=2 Severe=3 Severe, grossly disabling=4

Source: Hamilton M, 1959. Reprinted with permission.

her at her studies. At 22 the patient married the "first man that came along," and gave up her own career to devote herself to promoting her husband's acting career in New York City. After six miserable years of marriage, she returned home to Los Angeles in an attempt to put her "life together." Her husband followed from New York to try a reconciliation, but she felt helpless, trapped, and very confused. She was referred for psychotherapy.

In the first month of treatment, the patient had a panic attack on the way to a therapy session while driving on the freeway. Over the next five months she became increasingly agoraphobic, fearing to drive and afraid to leave home. She depended more and more upon her husband, became depressed, felt angry at herself, and experienced hopelessness about her condition. She feared that her psychotherapy was causing her "to get worse" in that she had felt better before starting therapy.

Treatment with imipramine, 75 mg at bedtime, was prescribed, and over the next four weeks the dosage was increased to 150 mg at bedtime. Meanwhile, psychotherapy was continued with the belief that many of the patient's symptoms could be understood on a psychodynamic basis. Gradually her symptoms subsided, and as the anxiety diminished she came to understand her feelings much better, i.e., her anger at her mother, her rage at her husband, and her disappointment in herself.

Abruptly, her husband left her for a younger woman who was a singer in San Francisco. The patient developed a new set of friends and relationships as her medication was gradually decreased. After six months, psychotherapy was discontinued.

The patient has seen her therapist from time to time during the past year. She remarried and has experienced no further panic attacks. She feels grateful for the psychiatric treatment she received, and claims that she has continued to benefit from the insight obtained in psychotherapy.

Phobic Disorder

The patient, a 37-year-old registered nurse with a history of phobias extending back 22 years, had been treated by a psychiatrist for 3 years beginning when she was 15 years old. During the 10 years following treatment, she continued to keep in touch occasionally, but after that, the patient's communications ceased. Coincidentally, the patient recently learned that the therapist she had seen as a teenager was editing a book on anxiety disorders, and she made an appointment to provide a 22-year followup of her phobia.

The woman was charming, clearly remembered by the therapist as a 15-year-old girl with her mother. At that time, she had presented with a phobia related to fear of eating meat, but she had a history of psychological problems in childhood. It seemed clear that she was the "identified patient" in a family that was in great distress. Her parents were having severe marital problems. Her mother had bathed her until the age of 12; her father walked around nude in the house, often sexually aroused; and there had been a great deal of family turmoil with an older sister.

Treatment of a patient like this today would probably involve the entire family in family therapy. Everyone in this family, however, was seen individually. The patient was treated by a psychiatrist. The mother was evaluated and eventually treated by a social worker, the sister was evaluated and treated by another psychiatrist, and the father was evaluated and treated by a clinical psychologist. Once a week, all four therapists met to discuss the dynamics of this family. At the completion of her treatment, the patient's phobia was somewhat diminished in intensity, although she was still quite anxious.

The followup of her disorder was both interesting and distressing. Following graduation from nursing school, she began experiencing panic attacks while driving her car. She had heard that behavior modification was useful for treatment of anxiety, and she consulted a behavioral therapist. During four sessions, however, she felt exploited and abandoned, and never returned. She then consulted a psychoanalyst whom she saw only once. He asked her whether she was orgasmic. She said that she had no difficulty experiencing orgasm. He reportedly said to her, "Well, I'll be darned, I've never before seen a person with anxiety hysteria who was orgasmic." (She expressed that "every time I have an orgasm I keep thinking of that guy.") However, this idea that she may have a sexual disorder led her to try a nude sexual encounter with the therapist-facilitator participating. None of these therapies helped her, and she became increasingly incapacitated and unable to work. During the late 1960s and early 1970s she experienced an average of five panic attacks in one day, and was literally confined to her apartment. Just at a time when the patient was hopeless and feeling suicidal, her symptoms miraculously subsided. Her phobias remained, but she was able to begin her nursing career, and, using a variety of antianxiety agents, was able to get through the day.

Three years previous to her followup, she learned in a newspaper article of imipramine in the treatment of panic disorders. She went to her family physician with the article and convinced him to begin an imipramine trial. For the first time in her life she became free of her incapacitating attacks. Recently, she learned of a new anxiety disorder clinic at a nearby university. She has been attending the clinic for six months and has just started on alprazolam, a medication which she feels has been of great benefit to her. She is now feeling very positive and optimistic.

The patient hoped that her experiences could be of help to other persons with anxiety disorders. She also expressed that she wanted to talk because she remembered the therapist was the person who tried to help her as an adolescent, and that caring for her meant a great deal to her. She stated, "The medication that I get from the university clinic is wonderful, but it doesn't help me as a 37-year-old woman to deal with my life. At the clinic they don't want to talk to me because I've had so much therapy. They just want to give me medication. Isn't it possible that someone can put the treatment together so that patients with anxiety disorders can have biological, family, psychodynamic, or behavioral approaches to fit their particular needs?"

Obsessive-Compulsive Disorder

The patient is a 45-year-old businessman who sought psychiatric consultation with the initial complaint of having trouble sleeping, frequently awaking in the morning with anxiety. He admitted that he had been complicating his difficulties with excessive drinking in the evenings. He was also having rather severe marital problems. He stated, "I am driving my wife crazy with my behavior."

During the first interview, he began rearranging the items on the psychiatrist's desk, lining up pencils, straightening the ashtrays, wiping dusty spots with Kleenex, etc. Finally, the patient revealed that his real psychiatric problem was his ritualistic behavior—he felt compelled to end a flight of stairs on his left foot. Because he was an excellent calculator, the patient could size up a flight of stairs and decide which foot to start with so that he could always end with his left foot on the top stair. In case of error, he experienced incapacitating anxiety.

He recounted a recent experience that began with him running to catch a plane to San Francisco. He was late and began running up the tail flight of steps of the Boeing 727, ending on his right foot. Although he sat down briefly and attempted to continue, he became so anxious with his fantasy that the plane would crash that he got up, running past the astonished stewardess and down the steps. He turned around and came up again, this time completing the flight of stairs on his left foot. As a result, he was able to continue his flight without significant anxiety.

The patient was treated for four months. He did not particularly want insight therapy; he readily admitted that he was really looking for "medication cure." Nonetheless, some limits and goals were set, including control of his alcohol intake and resolution of some of his marital problems. Treatment with phenelzine, 15 mg three times a day, with the usual dietary precautions was prescribed. It was hoped that within a few months he would be interested in obtaining some insight into his problems. He was not.

At the end of four months, following discontinuation of the medication, he left feeling much better. He had begun to work on some of the problems in his marriage, but had no desire for further treatment. It is likely that both he and his wife are still suffering from his compulsive ritualistic disorder.

Posttraumatic Stress Disorder

A 48-year-old medically retired Marine Corps officer was admitted for treatment of diabetic ketoacidosis. Because of the patient's difficulty in coping with situational crisis, a psychiatric consultation was requested on day 11 of hospitalization.

The initial evaluation revealed a history of chronic family discord. The patient had separated from his wife eight years before because "she still wanted to run the show" on his return from Vietnam. His most recent difficulty with her stemmed from a request that he help discipline their two sons. The patient had been unemployed for the previous three months. Although after returning from Vietnam he had earned a graduate degree, he described his last job as "a know-nothing" position. He volunteered no other information, but did ask the interviewer if he had been in Vietnam. When the interviewer said no, the patient dropped the subject.

At the second consultation two days later, the patient was specifically questioned about his combat experience in Vietnam and possible posttraumatic stress disorder (PTSD) aftereffects. He had served in Vietnam for six months, and heavy combat resulted in the loss of 500 of his men. He was one of only two officers to "leave the area alive." Except for marital discord, the patient denied having any immediate difficulty upon his return home. However, approximately two years after he had retired from the military, he noted increasing irritability and outbursts of anger. Other behavioral changes included nightmares involving combat, images of the war associated with certain stimuli (e.g., hearing a helicopter), marked estrangement from others, exaggerated startle response, survivor guilt, and chronic sleep disturbance. He was visibly disturbed by this factual recitation of his combat experience.

The patient reported 20 changes of address in the last few years and a loss of numerous jobs because of an ill-defined dysphoria. He denied carrying a weapon or suffering from paranoid ideation or from active, overt suicidal or homicidal ideation. Although the patient had sought the help of a veteran's therapy group one year earlier, he left the group after one month because of increasing anxiety and a need to talk on a "one-to-one basis." He did note a decrease in depression following this therapy.

This patient did not request a disability pension for his psychiatric problem. It is important to note that he actually denied symptoms of PTSD on admission and then failed to mention them at the initial psychiatric consultation as well. Only when questioned specifically did he reveal his inner torment (24).

Conclusion

Cases such as these illustrate the complexity of the clinical situations, the often overlapping nature of symptoms and disorders, and the problems in treatment. A clearer understanding of the biology of anxiety should promote the development of more effective preventive and therapeutic techniques, and help to separate out the various anxiety disorders. Anxiety is present in varying degrees in all psychiatric and physical illnesses. The clinician who possesses the requisite biological, psychological, and social knowledge will be capable of designing and implementing a comprehensive treatment approach based upon a thorough physical and psychiatric examination.

References

1. Boffey P: Anxiety: U.S. seeks improved insight into causes. N.Y. Times, p. C-1, Aug. 2, 1982

2. Beard M: Neurasthenia, or nervous exhaustion. Boston Med Surg J 3:217-221, 1869

3. DaCosta JM: On irritable heart: A clinical form of functional cardiac disorder and its consequences. Am J Med Sci 61:17-52, 1871

4. Oppenheimer BS, Rothschild MA: The psychoneurotic factor in the irritable heart of soldiers. JAMA 70:1919-1922, 1918

5. Cohen ME, Badal DW, Kilpatrick A, et al: The high familial prevalence of neurocirculatory asthenia. Am J Hum Genet 3:126-158, 1951

6. Noyes R, Clancy J, Crowe RR, Hoenk PR, Slymen DJ: The familial prevalence of anxiety neurosis. Arch Gen Psychiatry 35:1057-1059, 1978

7. Klein DF, Fink M: Psychiatric reaction patterns to imipramine. Am J Psychiatry 119:438, 1962

8. Crowe RR, Pauls DL, Slymen DJ, Noyes R: A family study of anxiety neurosis: morbidity risk in families of patients with and without mitral valve prolapse. Arch Gen Psychiatry 37:77-79, 1980

9. Raskin M, Peeke HVS, Dicman W, Pinsker H: Panic and generalized anxiety disorder: developmental antecedents and precipitants. Arch Gen Psychiatry 39:687-689, 1982

10. Hamilton M: Diagnosis of anxiety states, in The Biology of Anxiety. Edited by Matthew RJ. New York, Brunner/Mazel, 1982

11. Hartman N, Kramer R, Brown T, Devereaux RB: Panic disorder in patients with mitral valve prolapse. Am J Psychiatry 139:669-670, 1982

12. Uretsky BF: Does mitral valve prolapse cause nonspecific symptoms? Circulation 62:206, 1980

13. Pollitt J, Young J: Anxiety state or masked depression. A study based on the action of monoamine oxidase inhibitors. Br J Psychiatry 119:143-149, 1971

14. American Psychiatric Association: Diagnostic and Statistical Manual of Mental Disorders. Washington, DC, American Psychiatric Association, 1952

15. Bosselman BC: Neurosis and Psychosis. Springfield, Ill, Charles C. Thomas, 1950

16. Fenichel O: The Psychoanalytic Theory of Neurosis. New York, W.W. Norton, 1945

17. Rosenbaum JF: Anxiety: a psychiatric medicine update, in Psychiatric Medicine Update (1981 Edition),

Mass Gen Hosp Reviews for Physicians. New York, Elsevier, 1981

18. American Psychiatric Association: Diagnostic and Statistical Manual of Mental Disorders, 2nd ed. Washington, DC, American Psychiatric Association, 1968

19. American Psychiatric Association: Diagnostic and Statistical Manual of Mental Disorders, 3rd ed. Washington, DC, American Psychiatric Association, 1980

20. Hall RCW, Devaul RA, Stickney SK, Popkin MK, Faillace LA: Physical illness presenting as a psychiatric disease. Arch Gen Psychiatry 34:1315-1320, 1978

21. Rickels K: Drug treatment of anxiety, in Psychopharmacology in the Practice of Medicine. Edited by Jarvick ME. New York, Appleton-Century-Crofts, 1977

22. Parry HJ, Balter MB, Mellinger GD, et al: National patterns of psychotherapeutic drug use. Arch Gen Psychiatry 28:769-783, 1973

23. Hamilton M: The assessment of anxiety states by rating. Br J Med Psychol 21:50-55, 1959

24. Wise MG: Posttraumatic stress disorder: The human reaction to catastrophe. Drug Therapy, March 1983

2

The Psychobiology of Anxiety and Fear

Herbert Weiner, M.D.

2

The Psychobiology of Anxiety and Fear

Herbert Weiner, M.D.

Fear and anxiety play important roles in the everyday lives and in the survival of animals and human beings. Despite their biological significance in human behavior and in medicine, our knowledge of their physiology remains limited. Why should that be so? The answer is that persistent problems in their precise definition remain with us, and that the experimental study of anxiety in particular eludes us. Both phenomena are difficult to induce, control, and record experimentally.

Definition of Fear and Anxiety

All sentient creatures become alert and respond in an integrated psychobiological manner to threats to their survival, that is, to danger. Animals may also signal the presence of potential or actual danger to members of their own species, in particular to their relatives. Behavioral measures are then taken either to eliminate, avoid, or defend against the source of danger, to fight or to flee. Fear is the internal signal alerting the organism to external dangers.

We owe to Freud (1) the insight that the source of the threat or the danger may be imaginary or unrecognized. Anxiety, in his view, is an internal signal anticipating this danger, experienced as an unpleasant sense of foreboding, alerting the person to defend against or avoid it. The matter is not just this simple, however. Fear is also occasioned by an ambiguous situation, a contingency that also applies to anxiety. Additionally, a novel situation may be a potent inducer of fear.

Fear, Arousal, and Stress

Fear and anxiety alert and arouse the organism; they prepare it physiologically and stimulate it to act. But not all arousing stimuli, emotions, or exercise are frightening or anxiety-provoking. For example, a loud noise may startle, producing an orienting response; emotions such as joy, rage, sexual passion, and physical activity are also arousing. The claim that all emotional reactions should be conceived of in terms of a unidimensional concept of physiological arousal or activation is incorrect (2).

Many investigators prefer to subsume danger under the rubric of "stress"; immense and persistent difficulties remain with this word. Stress is too general a concept. Furthermore, it is unclear whether danger, anxiety, or fear are of necessity stressful. Many situations are recognized as being stressful but are by no means dangerous. For heuristic, experimental, and clinical reasons stress should be sharply separated from danger, fear, and anxiety.

Psychobiological Correlates

Physical activity and emotional arousal are associated with a variety of coordinated physiological changes. Even the anticipation of, or the preparation for exercise or the act of talking are accompanied by vasodilation, increased muscle blood flow, and increases in heart rate, blood pressure (3,4), and catecholamine secretion. However, attempts to define anxiety, fear, rage, and other emotions in terms of their associated or specific physiological responses have so far proved largely unsuccessful. Admittedly, increases in catecholamine excretion and turnover rates occur when subjects are frightened, but they also occur when subjects are understimulated by the environment (5,6); they appear to be mobilized by any *change* in the level of stimulation.

The biological function of fear and anxiety is adaptive— to alert the organism to a threat to its survival and to make it take appropriate action. At peak levels these signals may be pathological: they may paralyze or disrupt behavior and prevent appropriate action. But at moderate or modest levels they may promote learning by acting as motives of behavior. Some human beings court danger and have minimal physiological responses to it.

Individual Differences in Integrated Psychobiological Responses to Danger

Clinical experience alone informs us that anxious patients differ in their bodily symptoms and signs. Some patients experience marked increases in muscle tension in various regions of their bodies. A second group has mainly cardiorespiratory symptoms: changes in the rate and frequency of respiration and/or the rate and force of the heart beat. They may become aware of their heart pounding and beating more rapidly, or of an irregular beat. Another group of anxious persons will tremble, wring their hands, have dry mouths, experience upper abdominal sensations ("butterflies"), or they will vomit, have diarrhea, or an increased frequency of urination. A delay in the onset of sleep is also observed in many anxious patients.

Combinations of any or all of these symptoms may occur. These "response stereotypies" are also seen in the laboratory. Lacey (7) points out that different stimuli and contingencies produce similar responses in the same—but not in another—person. Hence, one source of differences between persons is the relatively characteristic pattern of physiological responses of individuals, without regard to the manner in which they are incited.

Conversely, the same frightening context produces

highly individual behavioral and physiological responses across groups of subjects. Where species differences are seen, individual differences of this kind also characterize the responses of groups of animals to danger.

These generalizations do not, however, exhaust the reasons for individual or group differences in the psychobiological responses to danger. They vary according to the following:

1. The novelty or the unpredictability of the situation.
2. The previous experiences the individual has had with the danger.
3. The role assigned to and carried out by the person in the situation of danger; whether, for instance, the role is as the leader or the follower.
4. The quality with which the role is performed: Does the person succeed or fail at it?
5. The manner in which the person copes with fear or defends against anxiety.

Methodological Problems in Studying Anxiety and Fear

The experimental study of anxiety has been fraught with a variety of serious problems. The induction, control, and measurement of anxiety in the laboratory remain unsolved, with the result that we know little about its physiology. In fact, most of the work reported in this chapter results from work on fear induced in naturalistic settings, which sets limits on gathering data and on the measurement and control of physiological variables.

Attempts to induce fear and anxiety in subjects in the laboratory have consisted of contrived situations designed to make subjects fearful, such as electrical shock or sparks. These experiments usually have been unsuccessful because subjects were not fooled by such simulated emergencies. Other experiments have attempted to simulate anxiety by injecting subjects with sympatheticomimetic drugs or lactic acid.

When anxious subjects are assessed psychologically by various tests and physiologically by recording various measures—pupillary size, cerebral blood flow or metabolism, salivary flow, heart and respiratory rates, cardiac output, blood pressure, blood flow through muscle and skin, sweating, gastric motility, or various blood levels of catecholamines, hormones and free fatty acids—low correlations are obtained between the two sets of measures (6). Hence, the most meaningful data have been obtained by studying subjects in the field—in dangerous situations such as combat training or actual combat, examinations, or frightening medical procedures. The drawbacks of this approach are that the situational variables are difficult to control and isolate, and the data are of a correlative, not an analytic, nature.

Experimental Laboratory Studies

Are fear or anxiety, studied in the laboratory, associated with different patterns of physiological change than are sadness, happiness, and anger? Schwartz and co-workers (8) used the technique of guided imagery to induce reminiscences and mental images associated with these four feelings in 32 subjects. These images were then re-created during a second period when subjects also were asked to imagine themselves walking up and down a step; during a control period; during a third period when subjects performed a step-test while again imagining the previous scenes and their associated feelings; followed by a neutral control condition while exercising.

Mean and diastolic blood pressure increments were significantly greater with anger than with fear. But increases in systolic blood pressure were the same for all four emotions. The heart rates of subjects rose in equal amounts with anger and fear, and were much greater than with images associated with feelings of happiness and sadness (Figure 2-1). When anger was combined with exercise, the greatest increases in heart rate and systolic blood pressure were achieved, and they returned to baseline levels slower than with any other emotion (Figure 2-2). In these experiments only anger was accompanied by distinctive cardiovascular changes. Fear produced no unique cardiovascular effects when compared with sadness and happiness.

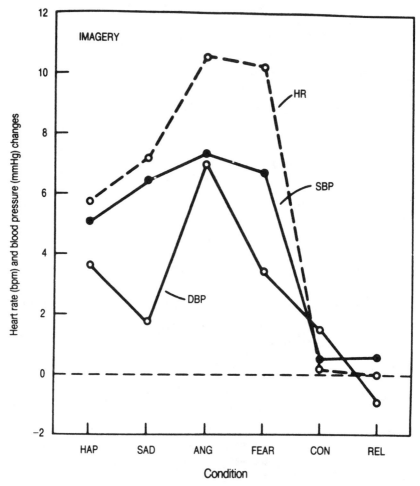

Figure 2-1. Mean changes in heart rate (HR) and in systolic (SBP) and diastolic (DBP) blood pressure separately for the happiness (HAP), sadness (SAD), anger (ANG), fear (FEAR), control (CON), and relaxation (REL) conditions following seated imagery.

Source: Schwartz et al., 1981. Reprinted with permission.

Yet by the use of electromyography, anger and fear can be discriminated. The former produces tonic, regular potential discharges and the latter phasic ones (9). These findings suggest that the potential changes in muscle prepare the angry person for a single sustained movement (a blow), but that in fear the muscle is ready for intermittent movements (running).

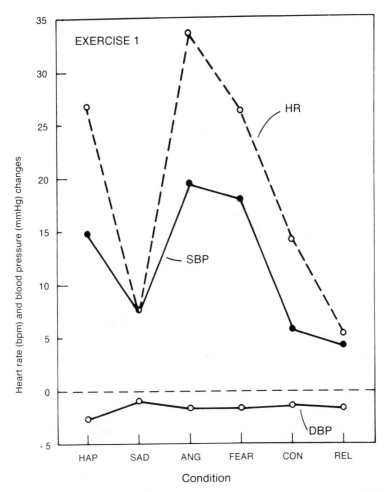

Figure 2-2. Mean changes in heart rate (HR) and systolic (SBP) and diastolic (DBP) blood pressure separately for the happiness (HAP), sadness (SAD), anger (ANG), fear (FEAR), control (CON), and relaxation (REL) conditions during the first measurement following exercise.

Source: Schwartz et al., 1981. Reprinted with permission.

Naturalistic Experiments

In Animals

Hofer (10) captured six species of wild desert rodents and exposed them to snakes and the silhouette of a hawk, their natural predators. Four of the six species—chipmunks, ground squirrels, wood rats, and grasshopper mice—became tonically immobile, a behavior of obvious survival value as retinal cells of the predator respond predominantly to moving objects. During the state of tonic immobility, their rate of breathing was increased fivefold. Although their heart rates showed little change, 56 percent of the animals had a variety of cardiac arrythmias—sinus, different degrees of atrioventricular block, and ventricular ectopic beats. Individual and species differences on these variables were prominent. In the two other species, the deer mouse and kangaroo rat, the heart rate rose 33 to 100 percent, but no arrhythmias were recorded.

Wild rabbits, on the other hand, develop "fright" hyperthyroidism after initially being trapped by ferrets, and when later again exposed to these predators or to dogs. Initially, they also become tonically immobile, tremulous, have marked increases in heart and respiratory rates, and develop exophthalmos. On reexposure to their predators, the rabbits begin to lose weight, show increases in radioiodine uptake, and eventually die. Antithyroid drugs or thyroidectomy avert the weight loss and death (11).

In Humans

Cardiorespiratory Changes. Training in the use of parachutes is a reliable way of inducing fear even in experienced jumpers. Fenz and Epstein (12) compared ten novice and ten experienced jumpers while rating fear, heart rates, respiratory rates, and skin conductance before, during, and after the jump from 5,000 feet (Figures 2-3 and 2-4). The novices were frightened to the point of being disorganized in thought and behavior; most of them found the first jump terrifying, while some others found it thrilling.

Among both experienced and novice jumpers, mounting anticipatory fear manifested itself in the bus on the way to the airfield. But in the experienced jumpers, fear declined at the point of maximum danger—when jumping out of the aircraft. During the actual fall, they were relatively relaxed. The novices, on the other hand, continued to experience mounting fear until they had landed. In both groups, respiratory rate was the first to increase, then the heart rate rose, and skin conductance fell. Among experienced

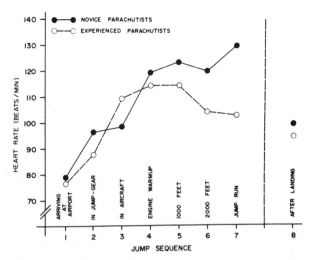

Figure 2-3. Heart rates of experienced and novice parachutists as a function of events leading up to and following a jump. Note the increases in heart rate in anticipation of the jump in experienced parachutists. The heart rates in the novices continue to increase in the aircraft and up to the point of the jump.

Source: Fenz and Jones, 1972. Reprinted with permission.

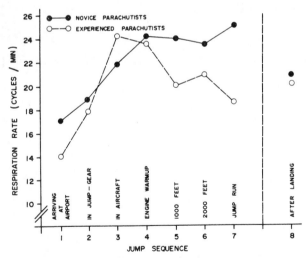

Figure 2-4. Respiration rate of experienced and novice parachutists as a function of events leading up to and following a jump. Note that the experienced jumpers show the greatest increments in rates prior to engine warm-up, following which the rates fall. In novice jumpers the rates rise, then plateau, only to increase somewhat at the time of the jump.

Source: Fenz and Jones, 1972. Reprinted with permission.

jumpers, the physiological changes peaked and then fell after they entered the aircraft, but among the inexperienced jumpers they continued to increase in the expected manner with the actual jump. Precise correlations between the fear self-ratings and the physiological changes occurred in the novices. Among the experienced jumpers a dissociation between fear and the physiological changes took place while preparing for and engaging in the jump.

Even experienced jumpers performed differently when rated by two jump-masters. Those who performed poorly had the greatest physiological changes. Their respiratory rates rose sharply until the point that the engines of the aircraft were warming up and then they plateaued, but their heart rates continued to increase until the jump was completed. By contrast, among the good performers the respiratory rates first increased then fell, and the heart rates plateaued (Figure 2-5).

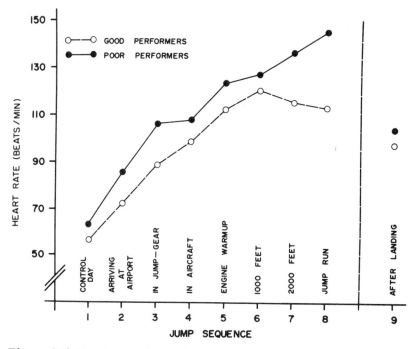

Figure 2-5. Heart rate of good and poor performers from among experienced parachutists as a function of events leading up to and following a jump.

Source: Fenz and Jones, 1972. Reprinted with permission.

The experienced jumpers who performed poorly, showed physiological patterns reminiscent of novice jumpers. It follows that the individual manner in which persons respond psychophysiologically to a frightening situation depends both on their experience and their performance at the time (13).

Catecholamines. The cardiac changes just described are mediated by adrenergic discharge. Recent developments now allow accurate techniques for the estimation of epinephrine and norepinephrine in serum, and these neurotransmitters have been measured in fear- or anxiety-provoking situations demanding performance (14,15). Among young physicians who had to make presentations at grand rounds, epinephrine levels rose sharply before and at the onset of the talk and then subsided during its course. Norepinephrine levels gradually increased and remained elevated throughout the period of the talk. Marked individual differences both in levels attained and patterns were observed. In some speakers the levels remained unchanged from the beginning to the end of the talk. The changes in catecholamine levels during the presentation differed from those seen during exercise, when norepinephrine levels alone increased.

3-Methoxy, 4-Hydroxy Phenylglycol (MHPG). Norepinephrine is metabolized to MHPG, and 25 percent of all MHPG in urine is believed to derive from brain norepinephrine stores. MHPG (but not urine volume) rose significantly in the pilots and radar officers of U.S. Navy jet fighters making aircraft landings. The highest levels were obtained in pilots during actual night landings, considered to be the most dangerous form of exercise; lesser increases in levels occurred during day landings. Simulated landings in a laboratory produced no changes in MHPG levels (16). (These patterns differ from cortisol changes in the same situation.)

Free Fatty Acids (FFAs) and Other Plasma Lipids. Changes in FFAs presumably are a measure of the mobilization of catecholamines, corticosteroids, and other hormones. They are readily measured in serum, and are exquisitely sensitive to a wide variety of contingencies, including those which are dangerous and anxiety-provoking (17). Their relevance in clinical medicine is that they have cardiotoxic effects.

FFAs begin to increase in anticipation of dangerous or anxiety-provoking situations. During examinations, however, only the most anxious medical students showed significant increases in FFAs (18). But among race car drivers, levels of FFAs rose (125 percent increases) before a race and peaked at the start. Triglyceride levels began to increase (111 percent) when the starter dropped his flag, and continued to do so for the first hour of the race (19). Patients faced with the novelty and fear of cardiac catherization uniformly had enhanced levels of FFAs before and throughout the procedure (20).

Cortisol and 17-Hydroxycorticosteroids (17-OHCS). During cardiac catherization, only the most overtly frightened patient had significant increases of serum cortisol—a traditional measure of stress, unpredictability, novelty, pain, and danger in humans. The frightened patients could be divided into two subgroups. Those who talked to the physicians about their concerns during the procedure showed no change in human growth hormone (hGH) levels, whereas those who did not had significant increases in hGH levels (Figures 2-6 and 2-7) (20).

Underwater demolition training and performance is one of the most dangerous situations known. Serum cortisol levels under these circumstances were consistently raised to three times normal levels (22 μg/dl). With the introduction of novel procedures or unfamiliar equipment during such training, further increases of serum cortisol levels occurred. As soon as the new equipment was mastered, however, these additional levels returned to steady, high basal levels (21).

Landing jet-fighter planes on aircraft carriers produces a high death or accident rate among pilots and their crews. The successful completion of any landing is always in doubt. Even experienced pilots are fearful, but they rated themselves as less frightened than the crewmen who operated the plane's radar equipment. Nevertheless, the pilots showed a threefold increase in serum cortisol levels (from 4 to 13 μg/dl). The greatest increments occured in pilots

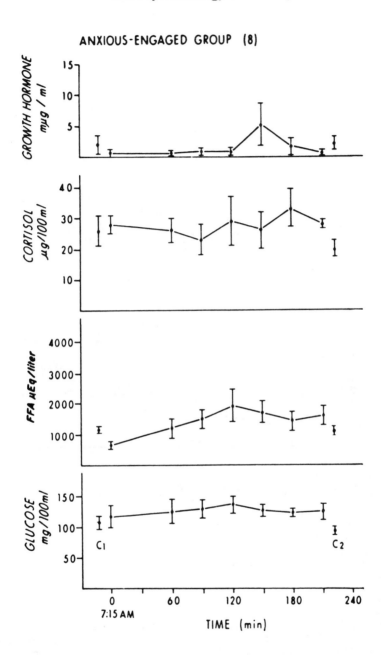

Figure 2-6. Levels of growth hormone, cortisol, FFA and glucose ($\bar{x}$ ± SE) at 7:15 AM at beginning (60 min), and every half hour during catherization in 8 patients who expressed their anxiety (anxious-engaged). C_1 and C_2 represent these levels ($\bar{x}$ ± SE) for 7:30 AM (C_1) and 11:00 AM (C_2) on comparative day before or after catherization.

Source: Greene et al., 1970. Reprinted with permission.

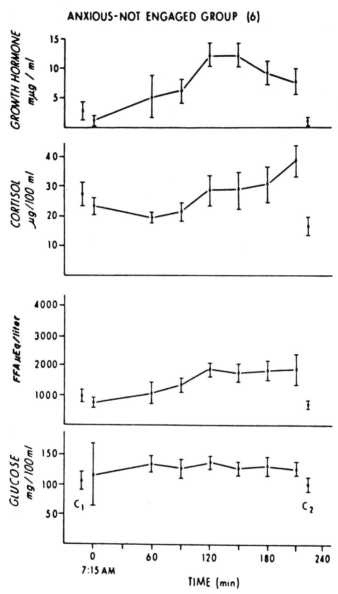

Figure 2-7. Levels of growth hormone, cortisol, FFA and glucose ($\bar{x}$ ± SE) at 7:15 AM at beginning (60 min), and every half hour during catherization in 6 patients who did not express their anxiety (anxious not engaged). C_1 and C_2 represent these levels ($\bar{x}$ ± SE) for 7:30 AM (C_1) and 11:00 AM (C_2) on comparative day before or after catherization. Note the differences in changes in growth hormone and serum cortisol levels and patterns in the two groups.

Source: Greene et al., 1970. Reprinted with permission.

Table 2-1. Mean Serum Cortisol Levels

Activity	Serum cortisol (μg)	Percent increase over control	Individual increases over control	t	df	p
Pilots						
Control	4.03 ± 1.64	—	—	—	—	—
Night MLP	8.95 ± 4.34	122	8/9	4.62	16	<0.0005
DAYQUALS	13.24 ± 6.00	229	9/9	5.61	16	<0.0005
NITEQUALS	9.21 ± 5.98	129	7/9	2.74	16	<0.01
RIO's						
Control	6.15 ± 3.39	—	—	—	—	—
Night MLP	5.22 ± 3.29	−15	5/10	0.74	18	NS
DAYQUALS	8.58 ± 4.99	40	6/10	1.32	18	NS
NITEQUALS	7.96 ± 4.11	29	7/10	1.02	18	NS

Note: Mean serum cortisol levels, standard deviations, *t* tests of differences between correlated means for control day compared with flying days, and one-tailed probabilities for pilots (N = 9) and radar intercept officers (N = 10) during simulated night mirror landing practice (MLP) on land, actual daytime carrier (DAYQUALS) and nighttime carrier qualifications (NITEQUALS). Note the increases in serum cortisol in the pilots only (even during simulated practice) despite the fact that actual landings are highly dangerous.

Source: Miller et al., 1970. Reprinted with permission.

during day landings, despite the fact that landing at night is more perilous. Even simulated landings in a laboratory were associated with a rise in cortisol levels in pilots. Therefore, the responsible individual secretes more cortisol in this situation (22) (Table 2-1).

Bourne and others (23) reached a similar conclusion while studying the experienced officers and men of a Green Beret combat unit in Vietnam when they were anticipating and experiencing a preannounced Viet Cong attack. The highest increases in levels of 17-OHCS excretion occurred in the two officers and in the radio operator. Actually, in the enlisted men, the levels fell during the attack and then returned to baseline levels (Figure 2-8). When other soldiers under fire are carrying out their customary duties and rituals with hope, or when resorting to prayer, seemingly oblivious to the threat of injury or death, they have lower urinary 17-OHCS levels than predicted by their body weight (24).

Hormone Patterns. This review, which is by no means exhaustive, has focused on the results of studies of dangerous situations and single dependent variables. A more

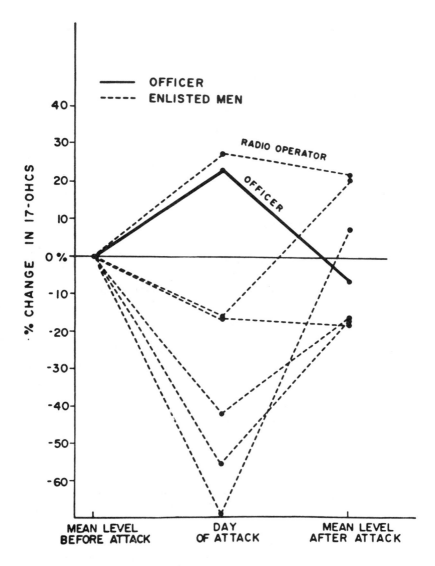

Figure 2-8. Percentage change in 24-hour urinary 17-hydroxycortico-steroid levels in an officer, radio operator, and 5 enlisted men before, during, and after a Viet Cong attack. Note the increased levels in the two former and the decreases in the five latter during the attack. Individual differences in levels are also notable.

Source: Bourne et al., 1968. Reprinted with permission.

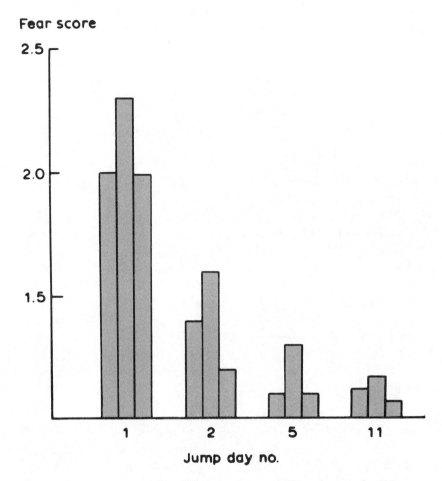

Figure 2-9. Self-rating of fear of men who went through parachute tower training. The three columns for each jump day represent the average scores at the bottom of the tower, those just before jumping and those just after the jump. Note the decreasing amount of fear with experience, and its anticipatory nature.

Source: Ursin et al., 1978. Reprinted with permission.

fruitful approach is to study the effects of danger and the attendant fear it induces on hormonal patterns. Ursin and his colleagues (2) carried out such a study on 44 young novice soldiers undergoing parachute training (Figure 2-9). The patterns of fear displayed were similar to those seen in Fenz's studies (12,13) previously reviewed. But Ursin and others reported that 13 of the 44 soldiers quit training after the first jump, during which they had experienced great fear, very high levels of epinephrine and norepinephrine, and elevated blood glucose, FFA, and testosterone levels.

The remaining 31 soldiers performed variably. The good performers were relatively unafraid and impatient to try the jump again, which they found thrilling. They had the highest FFAs and moderate epinephrine and norepinephrine increases during the jump. As they became increasingly adept the acute increases in these measures became less with each successive jump. Throughout the series their cortisol levels were low.

Those who performed poorly throughout claimed to be unafraid but had the largest rises in serum cortisol and hGH levels. Only minor increases in epinephrine, norepinephrine, and prolactin levels occurred. Those soldiers who ultimately failed the course had a rise in prolactin and a fall in testosterone levels (Figures 2-10 through 2-15).

These studies document that the novelty of a dangerous situation, the manner in which persons react psychologically to it, and the manner in which they perform in it determine the nature and the extent of the physiological responses.

Measures of Brain Function. The central nervous system correlates of fear and anxiety are poorly understood. There is general agreement that the electroencephalogram (EEG) is desynchronized, i.e., an increase in low-voltage fast activity (in the beta range) occurs and some theta waves (8-13 Hz) appear. The slow direct-current potential, called contingent negative variation, which can be recorded over the frontal regions of the skull, is a measure of the subject's expectancy or anticipation of a signal. In anxious patients its amplitude is diminished, the subject's expectancy of the occurrence of a signal is not maintained, that is, the subject is distracted from it (25).

Various techniques for measuring the cerebral circulation—blood flow and oxygen consumption—have been developed. Kety (26) used the nitrous oxide technique and showed by its use that anxious subjects had a cerebral blood flow 21 percent and a cerebral oxygen consumption 22 percent above calm subjects. With the xenon-inhalation

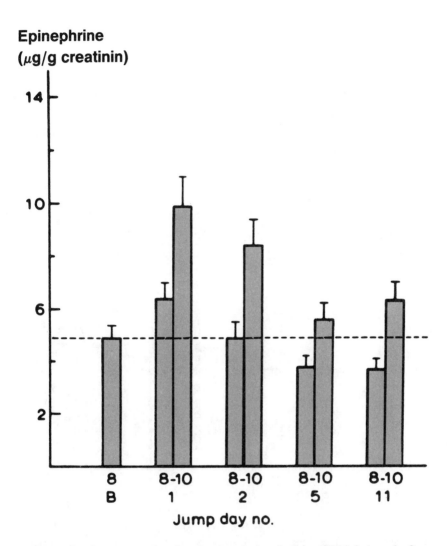

Figure 2-10. Urinary levels of epinephrine before (0800 hr) and after (1000 hr) the jump from the mock tower training apparatus. The vertical line on the top of each bar indicates the standard error of the mean. B = basal level obtained at 0800 hr. The broken horizontal line illustrates that the 0800 hr levels (pre-jump) gradually drop below the level obtained on the basal day. The highest levels of epinephrine levels occurred in those subjects who were most afraid and performed poorest.

Source: Ursin et al., 1978. Reprinted with permission.

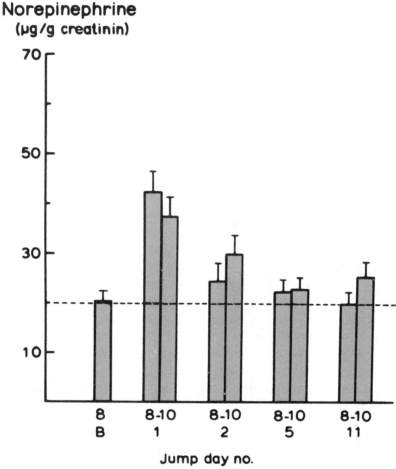

Figure 2-11. Urinary levels of norepinephrine before (0800 hr) and after (1000 hr) the jump from the mock tower training apparatus. The vertical line on the top of each bar indicates the standard error of the mean. B = basal level obtained at 0800 hr. The broken horizontal line illustrates that the 0800 hr levels (pre-jump) do not drop below the level obtained on the basal day. Note the differences in epinephrine (Fig. 2-10) and norepinephrine levels in the same subjects.

Source: Ursin et al., 1978. Reprinted with permission.

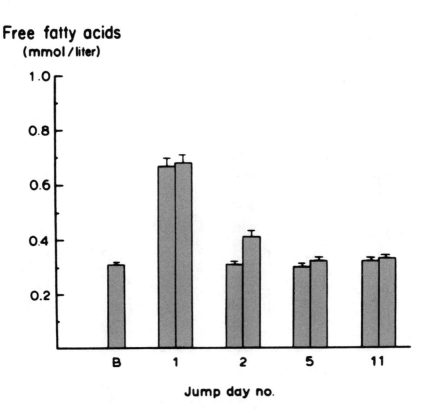

Figure 2-12. Plasma levels of free fatty acids. B = basal level. For each jump day two samples were obtained, one immediately after the jump and one 20 min. later. The vertical line on the top of each bar indicates the standard deviation of the mean. Note the decline in levels with experience.

Source: Ursin et al., 1978. Reprinted with permission.

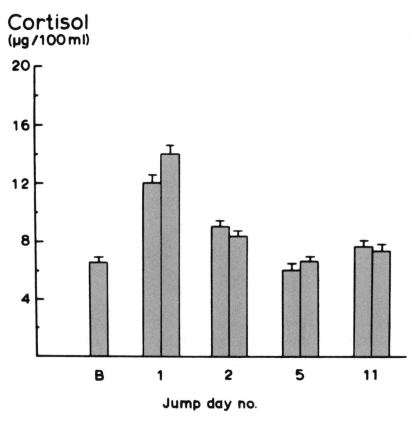

Figure 2-13. Plasma levels of cortisol. B = basal level. For each jump day two samples were obtained, one immediately after the jump and one 20 min. later. The vertical line on the top of each bar indicates the standard error. The largest increases in cortisol levels obtained in those who claimed they were unafraid but who performed poorly.

Source: Ursin et al., 1978. Reprinted with permission.

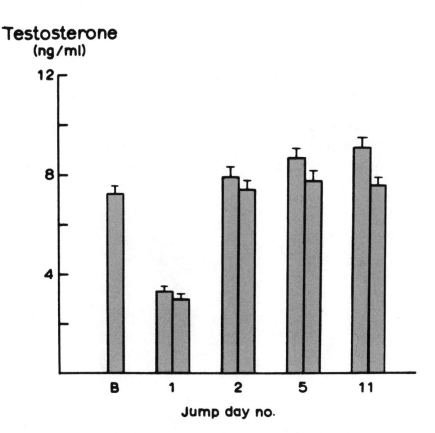

Figure 2-14. Plasma testosterone levels. B = basal level. Two samples were obtained on each jump day, one immediately after the jump and one 20 min. later. Note the abrupt fall on jump day number 1 when fear was the greatest. The most profound fall in levels were observed in the poorest performers.

Source: Ursin et al., 1978. Reprinted with permission.

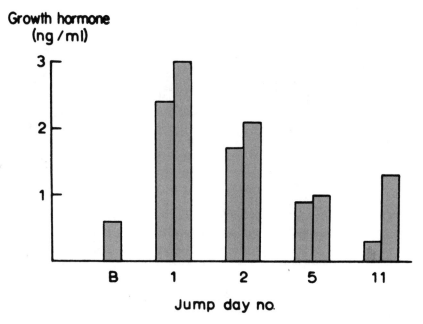

Figure 2-15. Plasma concentrations of growth hormone. B = basal level. For each jump day two samples were obtained, one immediately after the jump and one 20 min. later. Increases occurred despite increases in blood glucose levels (not shown). The largest increases in growth hormone levels occurred in men who performed poorly while claiming to be unafraid.

Source: Ursin et al., 1978. Reprinted with permission.

technique, which is newer and capable of measuring regional (mainly cortical) blood flow, anxious subjects showed some reduction of cortical blood flow, particularly in the right prefrontal, left prefrontal, both parietal, and right posterior temporal areas (27). These two techniques produce different results that are not easily reconciled.

The Neurobiology of Fear and Anxiety

We do not understand the neural basis of fear and anxiety. The arousing nature of both and the EEG changes described point to an increased activity of the midbrain reticular formation. Indeed, stimulation of upper midbrain structures produces pain mingled with fear. Upon electrical stimulation, the orbital frontal cortex, amygdala, and hippocampus seem to induce fear and anxiety in conscious subjects (28). Fear is generated in monkeys when the locus coeruleus is electrically stimulated. (This nucleus is the source of noradrenergic ascending axons.) After destruction of this nucleus, monkeys are rendered incapable of fear (29).

Our further understanding of the neurobiology of fear and anxiety is based on the logic that drugs that dampen them must act on neural structures that generate them. But drugs with many different pharmacological actions lower anxiety levels. The most fashionable of these are the benzodiazepines, which also have muscle relaxant, sedative, and anticonvulsant effects. Specific benzodiazepine receptors are located in the cerebral cortex, amygdala, corpus striatum, cerebellum, and spinal cord; two classes of these receptors have been discovered (30,31).

The benzodiazepines are functionally linked to gamma aminobutyric acid (GABA), an inhibitory neurotransmitter that promotes the influx of chloride ions into neurons, thereby hyperpolarizing them. Although they are not GABA agonists, the benzodiazepines potentiate its actions by removing an antagonist (31). Conversely, GABA potentiates the benzodiazepines by activating one of its two receptors. Additionally, the benzodiazepines slow the turnover of dopamine, norepinephrine, serotonin, and acetylcholine in the brain (32).

Receptor binding of the benzodiazepines is also influenced by stress, which is increased in rats repetitively shocked with electrical current. The binding is decreased when the drugs are chronically administered to rats that have not been shocked (33). By analogy with the opiate receptor system, the search is now on for an endogenous ligand that binds to benzodiazepine receptors. A number of candidate ligands have been put forward but none have been elected. The evidence is that GABA is not one of them. GABA has sedative and anticonvulsant properties, and it diminishes motor activity in animals, but it does not appear to reduce their fear (34).

The hypothesis that norepinephrine, acting centrally, may reduce fear and anxiety is based on the fact that clonidine—an alpha-2 receptor agonist—in low doses modestly lowers fear and acute panic attacks in humans. Individual differences in the effectiveness of clonidine is marked. Clonidine has sedative properties in humans, and it reduces acute but not chronic anxiety attacks (35). Imipramine, which increases the availability of norepinephrine at the alpha-2 receptor, may reduce panic attacks after a latent period of days or weeks (36). As yet there is no evidence that histamine, serotonin, dopamine, acetylcholine, various peptides, or adenosine are involved in either generating or minimizing anxiety and fear (32).

The fact remains, however, that anxiety in people is a heterogeneous phenomenon. Panic and chronic anxiety attacks do seem to respond to treatment with monoamine oxidase inhibitors and the tricyclic antidepressant drugs. On the other hand, acute anxiety attacks accompanied by enhanced muscle tension or autonomically mediated discharge to the heart, lungs, or gastrointestinal tract respond better to the benzodiazepines (37,38).

In summary, our ignorance of the mechanisms by which the brain signals danger with anxiety and fear is profound.

References

1. Freud S: The Problem of Anxiety. New York, Norton, 1936

2. Ursin H, Baade E, Levine S: Psychobiology of Stress. A Study of Coping Men. New York, Academic Press, 1978

3. Rushmer RF: Cardiovascular Dynamics. Philadelphia, Saunders, 1970

4. Weiner H, Singer MT, Reiser MF: Cardiovascular responses and their psychophysiologic correlates. A study in healthy young adults and patients with peptic ulcer and hypertension. Psychosom Med 24:477-498, 1962

5. Frankenhaeuser M, Nordeheden B, Myrsten AL, et al: Psychophysiological reactions to understimulation and overstimulation. Acta Psychol 35:298-308, 1971

6. Morrow GR, Labrum AH: The relationship between psychological and physiological measures of anxiety. Psychol Med 8:95-101, 1978

7. Lacey JI: Somatic response patterning and stress, in Psychological Stress. Edited by Appley M, Trumbull R. New York, Appleton-Century-Crofts, 1967

8. Schwartz GE, Weinberger, DA, Singer BA: Cardiovascular differentiation of happiness, sadness, anger, and fear following imagery and exercise. Psychosom Med 43:343-364, 1981

9. Ax AF: The physiological differentiation between fear and anger in humans. Psychosom Med 15:422-433, 1953

10. Hofer MA: Cardiac and respiratory function during sudden prolonged immobility in young rodents. Psychosom Med 32:633-647, 1970

11. Kracht J: Fright-thyrotoxicosis in the wild rabbit: A model of thyrotrophic alarm-reaction. Acta Endocrinol (Kbh) 15:355-362, 1954

12. Fenz WD, Epstein S: Gradients of physiological arousal of experienced and novice parachutists as a function of an approaching jump. Psychosom Med 29:33-51, 1967

13. Fenz WD, Jones GB: Individual differences in physiological arousal and performance in sport parachutists. Psychosom Med 34:1-18, 1972

14. Dimsdale J, Moss J: Plasma catecholamines in stress and exercise. JAMA 243:340-342, 1980

15. Taggart P, Carruthers M, Somerville W: Electrocardiogram, plasma catecholamines, and lipids, and their modification by oxprenolol when speaking before an audience. Lancet 2:341-346, 1973

16. Rubin RT, Miller RG, Clark BR, et al: The stress of aircraft carrier landings. II: 3-Methoxy-4-hydroxyphenylglycol excretion in naval aviators. Psychosom Med 32:589-597, 1970

17. Dimsdale J, Herd A: Variability of plasma lipids in response to emotional arousal. Psychosom Med 44:413-430, 1982

18. Bogdonoff M, Estes E, Harlan W, et al: Metabolic and cardiovascular changes during a state of acute central nervous system arousal. J Clin Endocrinol Metab 20:1333-1340, 1960

19. Taggart P, Carruthers M: Endogenous hyperlipedemia induced by emotional stress of race driving. Lancet 1:363-366, 1971

20. Greene WA, Conron G, Schalch DS, et al: Psychologic correlate of growth hormone and adrenal secretory responses of patients undergoing cardiac catheterization. Psychosom Med 32:599-614, 1970

21. Rubin RT, Rahe RH, Arthur RJ, et al: Adrenal cortical activity changes during underwater demolition team training. Psychosom Med 31:553-564, 1969

22. Miller RG, Rubin RT, Clark BR, et al: The stress of aircraft carrier landings. I: Corticosteroid responses in naval aviators. Psychosom Med 32:581-588, 1970

23. Bourne PG, Rose RM, Mason JW: 17-OCHS levels of combat. Special forces "A" team under threat of attack. Arch Gen Psychiatry 19:135-140, 1968

24. Bourne PG, Rose RM, Mason JW: Urinary 17-OCHS levels. Data on seven helicopter ambulance medics in combat. Arch Gen Psychiatry 17:104-110, 1967

25. Lader M: Biological differentiation of anxiety, arousal, and stress, in The Biology of Anxiety. Edited by Mathew RJ. New York, Brunner/Mazel, 1982

26. Kety SS: Circulation and metabolism in health and disease. Am J Med 8:205-217, 1950

27. Mathew RJ, Weinman ML, Claghorn JL: Anxiety and cerebral blood flow, in The Biology of Anxiety. Edited by Mathew RJ. New York, Brunner/Mazel, 1982

28. Nashold BS, Wilson WP, Slaughter G: The midbrain and pain, in Advances in Neurology, Vol 4. Edited by Bonica JJ. New York, Raven Press, 1974

29. Redmond DE, Huang YH: New evidence for a locus coeruleus-norepinephrine connection with anxiety. Life Sci 25:2149-2162, 1979

30. Tallman JF, Paul SM, Skolnick P, et al: Receptors for the age of anxiety: Pharmacology of the benzodiazepines. Science 207:274-281, 1980

31. Enna SJ: The role of neurotransmitters in the pharmacologic actions of benzodiazepines, in The Biology of Anxiety. Edited by Mathew RJ. New York, Brunner/Mazel, 1982

32. Hoehn-Saric R: Neurotransmitters in anxiety. Arch Gen Psychiatry 39:735-742, 1982

33. Grimm VE, Hershkowitz M: The effect of chronic diazepam treatment on discrimination performance and ^{3}H-flunitrazepam binding in the brains of shocked and non-shocked rats. Psychopharmacology 74:132-136, 1981

34. Palfreyman MG, Schechter PJ, Buckett WR, et al: The pharmacology of GABA-transaminase inhibitors. Biochem Pharmacol 30:817-824, 1981

35. Hoehn-Saric R, Merchant AF, Keyser ML, et al: Effects of clonidine on anxiety disorders. Arch Gen Psychiatry 38:1278-1282, 1981

36. Kahn RJ, McNair DM, Covi L, et al: Effects of psychotropic agents on high anxiety subjects. Psychopharmacol Bull 17:97-100, 1981

37. Muskin PR, Fryer AJ: Treatment of panic disorder. J Clin Psychopharmacol 1:81-90, 1981

38. Grunhaus L, Gloger S, Weisstrub E: Panic attacks: A review of treatments and pathogenesis. J Nerv Ment Dis 169:608-613, 1981

3

Anxiety and Physical Illness

Kenneth I. Shine, M.D.

3

Anxiety and Physical Illness

Kenneth I. Shine, M.D.

Introduction

Several years ago while I was making rounds on the coronary care unit, a new intern approached as I was talking with one of the residents. The intern patted me on the shoulder to get my attention. I turned to him as he said, "Dr. Shine?" I could hear his tongue peeling off the roof of his mouth as he talked. "Dr. Shine, there's a man in room 6 whose blood pressure is 65 and I don't know what to do." I had just been told about this patient by the resident, and as we walked into the room the nurse, who did know what to do, was drawing up some medication.

The patient was lying very stiffly in bed, staring at the ceiling. He was a 56-year-old man who had suffered an anterior myocardial infarction some two and a half days before. He lay there with bloodshot eyes, unshaven, and as we walked into the room, he made eye contact first with me and then with the intern who had just left his side. The terror in his eyes was reflected in those of the intern. The patient had a heart rate of 48 that was clearly a sinus bradycardia. I put my hands on his wrist, which had the effect of both confirming the pulse and making some physical contact with him, and I asked him what was wrong. "I am very tired," he said. "I haven't slept in two and a half days. I'm sure that if I fall asleep, I won't wake up." As we talked, the patient's pulse, which I was palpating, began to increase slowly in frequency and in amplitude.

I discussed with him the fact that we had made a mistake. Somehow we hadn't helped him to sleep, but there was reason why he couldn't go to sleep. We were monitoring him closely, his prognosis was improving rapidly, and the staff would quickly identify any problem that might develop. His pulse became fuller. The nurse was about to administer the atropine that she had drawn up, but I asked her to take the blood pressure again, and it was 85 systolic. After talking for just a few minutes the patient no longer needed any medication for hypotension or bradycardia. I have followed this man for seven years, and he has done very well after his anterior infarction.

This particular episode tells us a great deal about anxiety associated with acute illness. First, anxiety is part and parcel of a variety of physical illnesses but the manifestations of it may be very variable. Although we ordinarily anticipate that anxiety will manifest itself as a sympathetic discharge with a tachycardia, perhaps hypertension, and that it often will be associated with hyperventilation or paresthesias, anxiety also manifests itself in a variety of other physiologic ways, including bradycardia and vagal responses. Under certain circumstances, some individuals in a situation of stress or fear will have a vasovagal faint rather than become tremulous.

Second, it emphasizes that in the context of illness, anxiety can produce some extremely undesirable physiologic effects. Lack of sleep for two and a half days after an acute myocardial infarction limits the ability of the body to deal with an acute injury. Third, it emphasizes the importance of management of sleep in patients under these circumstances. Drs. Williams and Karacan cover this subject in great detail in Chapter 8.

Finally, and perhaps most importantly, this case demonstrates the interaction between the anxiety of the physician and the anxiety of the patient. One of the lessons I learned personally from Dr. Nemiah (and which he covers more fully in Chapter 5) is the importance of being sensitive to the feelings conveyed by the patient. One of the diagnostic clues to anxiety for the intern was the sense that he was becoming anxious in relation to his patient. In this particular case the interaction between the patient and the frightened intern, who actually performed very well, demonstrates the importance of dealing with these issues.

Anxiety and Cardiac Disease

There are many areas in medicine where anxiety interacts with physical illness. Most of this chapter, however, will focus on problems in patients with cardiac disease and particularly acute myocardial infarction.

Beginning in 1971, we developed a heart health care team as part of the coronary care unit at UCLA. This team included psychiatrists, psychologists, nurses, house staff, and others. Before discussing some of the problems that we have encountered, it is important to emphasize the way in which we have organized ourselves to deal prospectively with some of the problems and situations in which anxiety is a real signal of danger. For most patients there is no more dangerous or potentially fearful situation than the circumstances of an acute myocardial infarction.

One of the strategies we developed in the coronary care unit was the use of monthly, clinical, pathological death rounds, not only to allow the pathologist and the cardiologist to study the medical events, but also to have representation from the nursing staff. We reviewed those cases of patients who had died in the previous month and analyzed each case as to the level of care, whether the death could have been prevented in any way, or whether it was a nonpreventable death. Even when a death occurred three weeks before the death conference, staff was able to say to each other, "When things cool off, we're going to get together. We'll have our monthly conference and we'll analyze this." This discharged a tremendous amount of acute anxiety. People were able to return to work with the notion and the understanding that there was going to be a rational, arm's length review of what had happened. We found that this substantially reduced the anxiety among all the staff in our units, including the interns and residents. It became an important part of our monthly meeting aside from what we learned about the physiology of myocardial infarction. This is not to deny that acute support of staff was also required. These strategies not only helped the staff but also protected the patients from the impact of anxious personnel.

Cassem and Hackett have done a number of studies looking at events in the coronary care unit (1-4). They have developed indices to study the level of anxiety, depression, conflict, and what they call harmony among the staff in a coronary unit. Harmony was related to the ability of the personnel to work well together in relation to their mission. They determined these indices before and after the sudden death from ventricular rupture of a patient in the coronary care unit. Shortly after the death, the staff demonstrated an enormous increase in the level of anxiety. They showed a significant amount of increased depression, and conflict increased significantly among members of the group. A staff meeting was needed to discuss the problem, after which they were able to bring these parameters back to their pre-sudden death level.

Cassem and Hackett showed another interesting phenomenon. They described these same indices following cardiac arrest of a patient who was resuscitated as far as his heart was concerned, but who was brain damaged. There was a period of several days in which it was clear that he was terminal. This was again a great source of stress and anxiety in the coronary care unit. During this period the relationship among anxiety, the ability to work together, and depression was dissociated. The staff in this situation knew that the patient was going to die, and the level of anxiety was not particularly increased; however, their level of depression did increase substantially. They were now caring for a terminal patient whom they knew well. Interestingly enough, Cassem and Hackett pointed out this didn't necessarily interfere with the ability of people to work together. Harmony in the unit was enhanced (3). These findings have been confirmed in our experience as well. To the extent that we bring teams of people—physicians, interns, residents, and nurses—together in the care of these individuals, we sometimes enhance their working relationship.

It is also important to remember that we have to deal with the depressive aspects in addition to anxiety. Cassem and Hackett did a pioneering study of the various emotional responses of patients hospitalized after acute myocardial infarction as shown in Figure 3-1 (4). They observed that anxiety levels were maximal in the first 24 to 48 hours, and that over the next several days, anxiety began to diminish. During this time, the patients were building another defense mechanism, a kind of denial. It is not always clear whether this is a denial in a superficial sense or a psychoanalytical one, but patients increasingly behaved and talked as if little or nothing had happened to their health—

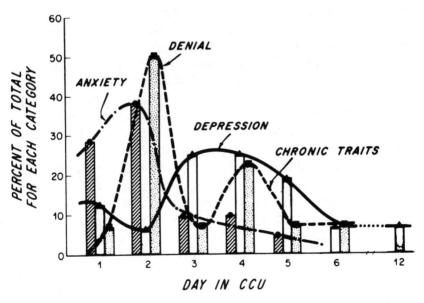

Figure 3-1. Emotional responses of patients hospitalized after an acute myocardial infarction.

Source: Cassem and Hackett, 1971. Reprinted with permission.

generally still complying with therapeutic recommendations.

When coronary patients first come to the hospital, often with pain, they are whisked into an emergency room, and into a coronary care unit. They are in fear of imminent death and this is a signal for appropriate anxiety. However, to the extent that their anxiety is dealt with, and particularly as symptoms decrease, anxiety levels tend to diminish. They develop additional coping mechanisms. By denial they tend to minimize the seriousness or significance of the event. Often, inexperienced individuals try to talk them out of this, to convince the patient of the seriousness of the problem. As long as patient behavior during this time is appropriate, however, denial is an appropriate defense with survival value. Survival may actually improve because heart rate and blood pressure are reduced and catecholamine release is minimized. Nevertheless, subsequently these patients often become depressed; the depression tends to appear during the second or third day after the infarction. Fuller recognition of the events that have occurred and future implications of the disease contribute to this depression, but anxiety usually persists.

During anxiety, free fatty acids are released, and there is evidence that these acids, which accumulate in the myocardium during infarction, are toxic. They produce arrhythmias and depress myocardial contactility. So there is reason to believe that controlling anxiety may have a direct physiologic effect upon survival. Cassem and Hackett also pointed out that later in the hospitalization behavior becomes much more influenced by the chronic personality characteristics of the patient during the premorbid history.

In our experience, anxiety is not necessarily limited to the first two days. It is usually most marked then, but there is a series of other anxiety states that occur in the natural history of an infarction. For example, separation anxiety is associated with the move from a coronary care unit to an unmonitored situation. We have developed graded care areas with intermediate care and progressive care, in part to deal with these issues. Sometimes it is difficult to move patients from a situation in which they believe that every heart beat is critically watched to a situation in which they are prepared to go home. Progressive care is very important to minimize the separation anxiety that reappears just prior to discharge for some patients and then reoccurs as individuals try to resume normal activities after they have left the hospital.

A Case Study

A 46-year-old physician had three hours of chest pain and, finally acceding to his wife, was brought to the coronary care unit. (Another person makes the decision for hospitalization for infarction in half of our patients.) Upon his admittance, the patient still had chest pain, his heart rate was 120, and he was tremulous, agitated, and convinced that he was about to die. A number of therapeutic responses can be made in this situation, including the use of sedation. Propranolol administered intravenously also can slow the heart rate and lower the blood pressure. This therapy often helps to achieve additional control of the anxiety because the patient no longer feels vigorous and rapid heart action.

In this particular case, suggesting Valium to the physician, who was very knowledgeable about the issues of myocardial infarction, created so much anxiety that he initially refused to accept any medication. One of the most anxious or anxiety-provoking issues for patients is loss of control during acute illness; there is no group more threatened by loss of control than physicians. Only after explaining to him the physiologic benefits that would accrue from slowing his heart rate and lowering his blood pressure, and enlisting his participation in the decision, did he agree. Subsequently, we did control his exuberant physiologic responses, and he was able to accept the notion that there was some physiologic benefit to his receiving some kind of sedation or tranquilization. But I emphasize again, for patients, issues of control have a great deal to do with anxiety. Therefore, in coronary care units we pay much attention to the patients' ability to control the environment including radio, television, bed position, movement to a chair early during convalescence, and similar maneuvers.

Anxiety of Medical Diagnosis

The natural history of myocardial infarction emphasizes some other aspects of anxiety and physical illness. Presentation to a patient of any medical diagnosis creates a certain amount of anxiety, the level of which may depend on a whole series of issues about which the physician has no knowledge. Our experience has been that the level of anxiety when giving a diagnosis is often so high that going from the diagnosis to a series of instructions about the illness may be unprofitable. This extends, on the one hand, from telling a patient that he or she has just had a heart attack and then entering into a complex discussion of the physiology of a heart attack, to telling an office patient that he or she has diabetes. That is not to say that one does not in fact make an attempt to explain what is going on to the patient, but the physician must understand that the patient often can't hear. The patient may be so preoccupied with the implications of the heart attack or the diabetes that the information must be repeated several times in the course of the illness.

Studies in the UCLA coronary care unit have shown that patients retain little information about their heart attack from that given during the first three or four days in the coronary care unit (5). The most effective educational program begins on day five, six, or seven, when the patient is out of the coronary care unit and in a position to retain information. One of the strategies behind this program includes the importance of early mobilization both for patients' physiological recovery and for reassurance and more control.

Anxiety of Medication

Patients must also be prepared for the anxiety aroused by going home. Cardiac patients face a series of new anxieties at that time; for example, the resumption of sexual activity. The patient is frightened and the spouse is often just as frightened. How does one deal with that? First, it should be dealt with prospectively. One has to present it to a patient in terms of the same physiologic parameters that have been addressed in the course of the patient's infarction. At the same time, a variety of tricks can be very helpful. For example, nothing may be more devastating than the patient's having angina in the course of the first attempt at sexual relations. Therefore, it becomes useful to give patients nitroglycerin prior to discharge and to have them administer it to themselves even though they've had no symptoms.

In our experience, so much anxiety is associated with the first self-administration of potent medication that it is critical for this to be done before the patient actually leaves the hospital. We routinely suggest that patients take a nitroglycerin before their first sexual encounter. Not only does this give the patient some notion that he or she can do something that will minimize difficulty, but it also has physiologic effects for prevention of symptoms.

This is also true of sleeping medications. Patients who have heart disease are afraid to give themselves a sleeping pill for fear that they'll be unaware of chest pains and not wake up. Again, therefore, it is important that they take the medication themselves just before discharge and find out that they can have a normal sleep.

Hyperventilation

In their work, internists see a significant number of patients whose anxiety disorder causes hyperventilation, which may in turn lead to the development of physical symptoms. These symptoms include paresthesias of the fingers, toes, and face; vertigo; and syncope. Usually the patient is unaware of the hyperventilation and is convinced that a serious heart attack or stroke may be occurring. To make the diagnosis and reassure the patient at the same time, it may be useful to reproduce symptoms. The technique is very straightforward. If the physician is suspicious that a patient's symptoms include a large component of hyperventilation, for example, with chest discomfort or paresthesias, or dizziness, it is relatively straightforward to say to a patient, "I'd like to check your heart rate and blood pressure when you are breathing rapidly,"—without making any further comments in regard to the patient's reported symptoms. The hyperventilating patient will spontaneously report the onset of these symptoms. This is extraordinarily useful, not only diagnostically but also to the patient. The physician can now identify that there may be organic reasons why the individual may get anxious, but certainly that some component of symptoms are related to this phenomenon which has just been demonstrated.

Mitral Valve Prolapse

An increasing source of anxiety for both patients and physicians is prolapse of the mitral valve. Patients with mitral valve prolapse appear to have unusual degrees of anxiety or neurosis (6), but because of the anxiety likely to be developed when the diagnosis is made, it is difficult to determine to what extent this is actually the case. Moreover, a significant selection process takes place if a patient who appears to be psychoneurotic or anxious presents to the physician. The physician's response may be to search for organic causes, including mitral valve prolapse. In my experience, far more anxiety has been elicited by medical contact than existed prior to the diagnosis of mitral prolapse and its prognostic implications. Although in some cases it is a serious disorder, these cases can ordinarily be identified clinically.

As experience develops we can place the disease into a more balanced perspective. From 6 to 18 percent of the normal female population has some degree of mitral valve prolapse (6). In some series, the number of males is comparable (7). Concerns about prolapse have arisen from instances of sudden death, presumably from arrythmias, as well as from the risk of endocarditis or progressive mitral regurgitation. Many of these patients have atypical chest pain and undue amounts of anxiety, and recent evidence shows an increased incidence of cerebral embolization (8).

Fortunately, the patients with highest risk can be identified in a relatively routine way. These patients have a click in midsystole followed by late systolic murmur, and their electrocardiograms show ST or T wave abnormalities or prolongation of the QT interval. Some of these patients have a family history of sudden death. Individuals who do not have a click or murmur or who have a perfectly normal electrocardiogram run an extremely small risk of serious complications. In such patients an extensive workup using Holter monitors, echocardiograms, and stress tests serves only to heighten the patient's anxieties. This workup is indicated only if the abnormalities noted above are observed. However, patients with mitral valve prolapse must be informed of its presence and instructed about antibiotic prophylaxis for dental and other minor surgical procedures.

Thyrotoxicosis

Thyrotoxicosis is another medical illness that may present as anxiety, nervousness, or weight loss, and with a series of functional complaints including rapid heart rate and diarrhea. Resting tachycardia, goiter, heat intolerance, and prominent stare are among the physical findings likely to identify thyrotoxicosis under these circumstances. The T4 index is a sensitive and effective screening test that will identify almost all cases of thyrotoxicosis except for those self-induced by administration of T3.

Neuromuscular Disorders

A variety of neuromuscular disorders can present primarily with fatigue and lethargy, and in some cases with an overlay of anxiety. Myasthenia gravis can be particularly anxiety invoking because of its intermittent occurrence and elusiveness of diagnosis. Inability to carry on sustained muscular activity and particularly to maintain a sustained upward gaze is usually a clinical clue to its presence. Suspicion of this disorder should lead to prompt neurologic assessment and consideration of a Tensilon test or some variant thereof. Polymyositis can be associated with weakness in various muscle groups, particularly of the proximal lower extremities. Inability to climb stairs or rise quickly from a chair gives an early clue to the presence of polymyositis. Such patients commonly have an increased erythrocyte sedimentation rate, increased creatine kinase levels in the plasma, and may have involvement of the skin as in dermatomyositis. Muscular dystrophies can occur in adults, producing progressive weakness. These are most commonly associated with wasting of the muscles in the shoulder and neck area or in the proximal thighs.

Pheochromocytoma

Pheochromocytoma, though a rare diagnosis, can also present with significant anxiety. In addition to hypertension, with its attendant symptoms of headache and sometimes visual disturbances, sweating is a particularly important symptom in pheochromocytoma. The appearance of paroxysms of headache and sweating should lead to careful checks of the blood pressure at that time. There are rare patients with epinephrine-secreting pheochromocytomas who actually have hypotension during such attacks. Suspicion of these disorders can be followed up by either plasma or urinary catecholamine determinations.

Conclusion

The relationship between illness and anxiety is confirmed in clinical practice every day by physicians in all specialties. Anxiety can present to a physician as a series of physical complaints. It can precipitate or exacerbate disease, and is an important concomitant of acute illness. But most important from the physician's point of view, anxiety may interfere substantially with the ability to rehabilitate the patient. Therefore, prospective and planned approaches are critical. Because anxiety among health professionals may also play a role, it follows that strategies involving consultative liaison with psychiatrists must deal not only with the patient, but also with the individuals who are caring for the patient.

References

1. Hackett TP, Cassem NH: Factors contributing to delay in responding to the signs and symptoms of acute myocardial infarction. Am J Cardiol 24:651, 1969

2. Cassem NH, Hackett TP: Psychological rehabilitation of myocardial infarction patients in the acute phase. Heart Lung 2:382, 1973

3. Cassem NH: What is behind our masks? AORN J 20:79, 1974

4. Cassem NH, Hackett TP: Psychiatric consultation in a coronary care unit. Ann Intern Med 75:9, 1971

5. Rahe R, Scalzi C, Shine KI: A teaching evaluation questionnaire for postmyocardial infarction patients. Heart Lung 4:759-766, 1975

6. Devereux RB, Perloff JK, Reichek N, et al: Mitral valve prolapse. Circulation 54:3, 1976

7. Ruthen DL: Non-rheumatic mitral regurgitation in the practice of cardiology, in The Practice of Cardiology. Edited by Johnson RA, Haber E, Austen WG. Boston, Little Brown, 1980

8. Hartman N, Kramer R, Brown T, Devereux RB: Panic Disorder in patients with mitral valve prolapse. Am J Psychiatry 139:669-670, 1982

4

Posttraumatic Anxiety

Louis Jolyon West, M.D.
Kerry Coburn, Ph.D.

Posttraumatic Anxiety

Louis Jolyon West, M.D.
Kerry Coburn, Ph.D.

Introduction

When you're lying awake with a dismal headache
and repose is taboo'd by anxiety
I conceive you may use any language you choose
to indulge in, without impropriety.
　　　　—Sir William S. Gilbert (Iolanthe, 1882)

Anxiety is a ubiquitous term. Coming to us from the Latin (anxietudo, anxietatem, anxius) it has for centuries carried several meanings in colloquial English. The original meaning clearly implies fear, apprehension or dread, also having a painful quality (*angst*). (E.g., c. 1525, Sir Thomas More, "There dyed he without grudge, without anxietie"; or 1631, John Donne, "Temporal prosperity comes always accompanied with much anxiety.") Another common use is of solicitude or concern; still another, eagerness (1742, R. Blair, *Grave*, 94, "The gentle heart, anxious to please"). In behavioral psychology anxiety often is used synonymously with fear as a classically conditioned mediating variable, motivating and reinforcing avoidance responses in accordance with 2-factor theory. In the poetry of psychoanalysis, anxiety permeates many verses as a major theme, wearing many personnae and sharing both salutary and pathological properties. And in the general parlance of dynamic psychiatry, pathological anxiety acquires its key differentiation from the parent emotion, fear, by the disguise of its cause. Fear is a normal mental, emotional, psychophysiological response to an identified genuine threat; anxiety is a similar response to an unknown threat. The fear response to a known but inappropriate or unrealistic threat or situation is called a phobia.

These many uses of the term anxiety become problematic when an attempt is made to derive general principles by comparing studies. As James Cattell wryly put it long ago, emotion represents such a large part of life (and, we would add, clinical literature), but such a small part of science. Much of this problem derives from a failure of many clinical investigators to designate unequivocally the objective criteria whereby they identify anxiety; in other words, a failure to come to grips with the purely definitional requirements of the language of science (1).

Because mental events are experientially different from physical events, it is unreasonable to suppose that a strict isomorphism exists between anxiety and the behavioral criteria used to describe it. For the psychoanalyst the problem can be particularly knotty when unconscious anxiety, which cannot be verbalized, is postulated as causative of a clinical symptom or pathological behavior that is not seemingly fearful. For the purpose of science, however, some replicable, observable, measurable, defining index is required ultimately.

This certainly does not imply that clinical investigations are not worthwhile. Quite the contrary, the clinician can venture into abstract areas of human existence unapproachable or only trivially approachable by animal experimentation; can identify problems and point to processes, states, and traits warranting further investigation; and can achieve fruitful insights without recourse to the cumbersome, grinding, numbercrunching methodology of laboratory methods. The most fruitful scientific pathway between the laboratory and the clinic, in psychopathology as in microbiology, is necessarily a two-way street.

For these reasons, both the clinical and the (laboratory) experimental literatures on posttraumatic anxiety will be employed in this discussion: the clinical to point the way; the experimental to explore the validity and reliability of candidate hypotheses. The clinical studies by Spitz and the experimental studies by Harlow on depression in infancy come to mind as an exemplar.

The term "traumatic anxiety" has been used to describe situations in which overwhelming anxiety is both the result and the cause of psychic trauma. "When it reaches paralyzing levels, anxiety no longer functions as a signal of danger but becomes a source of danger in its own right and is then designated traumatic anxiety" (2). The terms "traumatic anxiety" and "posttraumatic anxiety" are more usually employed to refer to the consequences of traumatic experience: anxiety is generated by physical or mental trauma and is experienced for some time thereafter. The present discussion uses the term in its latter sense, and thus is particularly (but not exclusively) concerned with the anxiety manifesting itself in the context of the posttraumatic stress disorder (PTSD) as defined by the third edition of the Diagnostic and Statistical Manual of Mental Disorders (DSM-III) (3).

Posttraumatic Stress Disorder

PTSD is very similar to what used to be called traumatic neurosis. The experience of two world wars demonstrated that healthy young men manifesting no previous psychiatric pathology could be severely debilitated by exposure to severe environmental stress even without physical injury. Cause and effect, at least at a molar level, seemed clear. Traumatic neurosis paralleled the military diagnoses of shell shock, operational fatigue, combat fatigue, combat exhaustion, and the like. PTSD is the latest and most systematic form of this long-recognized type of disorder.

Prior to the publication of DSM-III, aspects of psychoanalytic theory were cited to dispute the concept that stress in adult life could cause a neurosis; only childhood conflicts relating to the oedipal conflict could do that, later experience could act only as a precipitating factor (4). This limited concept about precipitation of latent neurosis had profound implications, even to the point of being used to deny the claims of holocaust victims for reparations. It also had important implications for veterans, whose eligibility for care at Veterans Administration hospitals depended in part on proof that a condition was service connected. Van Putten and Emory concluded their study of long-term psychological damage in Vietnam War veterans by noting, "It would appear that much of what has been learned about traumatic neurosis in World Wars I and II has been forgotten and needs to be relearned" (5). The 1980 publication of DSM-III has gone far toward remedying this unfortunate situation, especially by formalizing the diagnosis of delayed (posttraumatic) stress reaction, with symptoms appearing more than six months following the causative stress.

According to DSM-III, to diagnose posttraumatic stress disorder, four major criteria should be met:

1. The first criterion is, "the existence of a recognizable stressor that would evoke significant symptoms of distress in almost everyone." This seems to imply the existence of a class of universal stressors, which may not in fact exist. It is certainly appropriate to include in this criterion life-threatening experiences or other situations in which the victim feels utterly helpless to prevent severe injury or death (e.g., coercive interrogation and torture while in captivity). Experience with Vietnam returnees has convinced the Veterans Administration of the need to expand this category somewhat to include at least one situation in which the victim is in absolutely no physical danger—graves registration detail, which involves handling corpses, and has proved to be a significant stressor occasionally leading to PTSD.

In clinical practice it should be remembered that there are situations that may be extremely stressful to certain individuals without being "universal"; the *meaning* to the patient of the stressful situation must be assessed with great care. For example, the movie "The Exorcist" was reported to have caused traumatic "cinema neurosis" in at least four viewers (6) but left millions unaffected.

2. The second major criterion is a "reexperiencing of the trauma as evidenced by at least one of the following: (1) recurrent and intrusive recollections of the event; (2) recurrent dreams of the event; (3) sudden acting or feeling as if the traumatic event were reoccurring, because of an association with an environmental or ideational stimulus." This is an appropriate diagnostic criterion, but, in my experience, it is not inevitable. Although most people who have a posttraumatic stress disorder do indeed experience flashbacks, nightmares, and intrusive recollections, there are some who have only a dreamlike recollection of the trauma, and a few who experience partial or (very rarely) total amnesia for it. In such cases retrieval of the traumatic memory may come only as a consequence of therapeutic intervention. All the rest of the syndrome may be present after trauma, except for this item.

3. A third major criterion is "numbing of responsiveness to or reduced involvement with the external world, beginning some time after the trauma, as shown by at least one of the following: (1) markedly diminished interest in one or more significant activities; (2) feeling of detachment or estrangement from others; (3) constricted affect." A number of these cases have been particularly well described by Horowitz and Solomon in Vietnam veterans, and the numbness occurring in some posttraumatic syndromes is very prominent (7). It appears almost as though the ability to feel emotions has been exhausted, that the source of emotionality has been worn out. Such a reaction was powerfully portrayed by the actor Rod Steiger as a concentration camp survivor in a film called "The Pawnbroker." There were many such cases from POW camps and concentration camps. It should be kept in mind that such numbing of responsiveness, or reduced involvement with the external world, can come about as a result of experiences much less dramatic than concentration camps or combat.

Numbing can also reverse itself very rapidly during the course of treatment. For example, a person whose complaints are vague, and whose emotionality appears quite diminished, is prescribed a mild antidepressant for his apathy. The picture suddenly reverses itself, and a full-blown panic reaction explodes as the numbing defense fails, releasing a flood of dammed up emotions stemming from the trauma.

4. Finally, DSM-III requires "at least two of the following symptoms that were not present before the trauma: (1) hyperalertness or exaggerated startle response; (2) sleep disturbance; (3) guilt about surviving when others have not, or about behavior required for survival; (4) memory impairment or trouble concentrating; (5) avoidance of activities that arouse recollection of the traumatic event; (6) intensification of symptoms by exposure to events that symbolize or resemble the traumatic event."

The hyperalertness and exaggerated startle response were noted during the Civil War, but perhaps most vividly during World War I, when they were considered symptomatic of "shell shock." They were still with us in the "combat fatigue" of World War II, in the Korean conflict, in the posttraumatic stress disorders of Vietnam veterans, and in many patients after fires, earthquakes, automobile accidents, muggings, rapes, and a wide variety of other traumatic events. The sleep disturbances can be of various kinds, and are discussed elsewhere. Nightmares and night terrors are very common, and the anxiety that accompanies them may be so great that patients deprive themselves of sleep by fearing to return to bed after the nightmare wakes them.

Guilt about surviving while others have not is widely found among all kinds of survivors, including former concentration camp prisoners, combat veterans, victims of flood, fire, or airline crash, and torture victims. It is particularly intense when the patient believes that he or she behaved less than heroically, or otherwise failed to meet some personal standard. Memory impairment is not uncommon and ranges from a patchy amnesia to a well-delineated block of recall. The former is the more common, and can be very refractory to treatment.

Chronic impairments of memory and concentration may themselves cause great apprehension, including fears of insanity.

Avoidance of activities that arouse recollection of the traumatic event has been noted, especially in combat veterans. When seen in isolation, this symptom may lead to the diagnosis of phobia, although the original danger was external and very real. A similar problem is encountered with the intensification of symptoms—especially of anxiety—by exposure to events symbolizing or resembling the original trauma. This symbolization is not to be understood in the same context as that deriving from the concept of symbolization as defense, or as experienced in dreams.

DSM-III restored a legitimate diagnostic statement of the consequences of trauma, the posttraumatic stress disorder, in which acute, chronic, and delayed syndromes of anxiety and related symptoms occur. However, it seems likely that posttraumatic syndromes occur in even greater variety than the DSM-III criteria define. Many types of psychopathology can be precipitated by physical as well as mental trauma, not excluding severe illness or accidental injury (as in the case of Howard Hughes). Furthermore, severe physical or mental trauma (or both together) may precipitate many types of psychopathology, ranging from psychophysiological disorders to acute psychotic episodes. Nevertheless, the DSM-III diagnosis of posttraumatic stress disorder, with its emphasis upon anxiety-related symptoms and dissociative defenses, certainly encompasses the large majority of cases.

Trauma in Civilian Life

In many ways, trauma experienced outside the circumstances of war, concentration camps, torture in prisons and the like, might be expected to produce relatively pure examples of posttraumatic anxiety, uncluttered by many extraneous and probably interacting variables of military life.

Traumas affecting single individuals (e.g., rape, assault, accidents), groups (e.g., fires, airline or train crashes, shipwrecks) or populations (e.g., floods, hurricanes and tornadoes, earthquakes) tend to be episodic in their occurrence, and followed by prompt medical care when physical injury has occurred. Even large-scale calamities tend (in Western industrialized countries) to be limited in time, eliciting responses from disaster relief agencies which mitigate long-term effects of physical damage. In such cases of civilian trauma the afflicted individuals themselves will soon be fed and rested, and their physical injuries treated, thus restoring them in many important ways to the general state of the population.

Another advantage of studying posttraumatic anxiety in civilian populations is that the type and source of trauma do vary over several specifiable dimensions. In principle, this characteristic should allow the data to be analyzed as multifactoral "natural experiments," although in practice our efforts have lagged far behind such ambitious aspirations.

The assertions of White and Haas that no broad base of knowledge has emanated from research on natural disasters, and that early research findings have not been updated with respect to the social and economic changes occurring in the United States, still hold a large measure of truth nearly a decade later (8). The field of civilian trauma in general, and civilian psychological reaction to natural disaster in particular, has an unfortunate history of overgeneralization on the basis of biased and selected samples, and is only now beginning the transition from informed speculation to empirical research.

As Fredrick recently pointed out, older disaster studies tended to focus on sociological, or economic, rather than psychological factors influencing disaster recovery (9). Such studies often reported that flagrantly deviant behavior (such as grossly psychotic, berserk, or panic reactions) occurred only rarely or under special circumstances. Subsequently, the general climate of informed opinion inclined toward the view that the mental and emotional effects of disaster were likely to be both minimal and transitory. Emphasis was placed on reports of group cohesiveness and heroic acts during the "impact" period, community euphoria during the following "honeymoon" period, turning to resentment and frustration during the "disillusionment" period, and finally moderating to cautious optimism during the "reorganization" period. The focus was upon generally adaptive and situationally appropriate group efforts to cope and rebuild, frustrated by bureaucratic delays or social impediments rather than by individual psychopathology.

From a mental health perspective, such studies were narrow and parochial and of an inadequate design for reliable conclusions to be drawn. Greater understanding came with more sophisticated studies following certain disasters of the seventies: the San Fernando earthquake (1971), the Buffalo Creek flood (1972), the Grand Teton flood (1976), the Kentucky Supper Club fire (1977), the San Diego airline crash (1978), the Massachusetts blizzard (1978), and the Three Mile Island nuclear accident (1979). The research involvement of clinical investigators who were mental health professionals led to the realization that significant psychological disturbance may indeed be found in a large proportion of disaster (or similar trauma) victims, and that such mental and emotional symptoms may be amenable to crisis intervention, short-term counseling, group therapy, or even more prolonged dynamic psychotherapy in some cases.

Inevitably, most of these studies remain descriptive and qualitative in nature, pointing out the existence of significant mental health problems in the wake of disaster, but relatively lacking in quantitative or analytical data. However, now that the problem has been identified by clinicians and recognized by Congress in the Disaster Relief Act (Public Law 93-288), we may anticipate that well-designed studies using both cross-sectional and longitudinal approaches coupled with multivariate analyses will be forthcoming. For the moment, we must rely on clinical observations deriving from a largely anecdotal database.

A commonly cited estimate holds that roughly 25 percent of the population affected by a natural disaster may be expected to behave "efficiently" during the immediate posttraumatic period. Another 25 percent will show clearly inappropriate and disturbed responses of one sort or another. The remaining 50 percent will fall somewhere between these two extremes (10-12). Melick and co-workers state that experience shows at least 15 percent of the afflicted population will suffer from mental distress severe enough to require treatment (13).

The most frequent aberrant behavior of victims during the postimpact period has been described as a "shock" reaction, and appears to be similar to the immediate reaction to combat trauma. Coleman and co-workers described three stages of reaction to disasters in civilian life, beginning with an initial shock stage during which victims appear stunned, dazed, and apathetic (14). Victims may wander aimlessly unless guided or directed, and are unable to make more than a minimal effort to help themselves or others. In severe cases victims may be stuporous, disoriented, or amnesic. This shock stage is viewed as evidence of psychological decompensation, during which victims are protected by primitive defenses against the full impact (presumably overt anxiety, panic, anguish, grief) of the trauma until it can be assimilated. The presence of anxiety in this early posttraumatic period is often inferred for theoretical reasons, but its actual measurement is problematic.

The shock stage is usually followed by a "suggestible stage" in which victims are passive and cooperative. While expressing extreme concern for others and attempting to assist rescue workers, they tend to be inefficient in the performance of even routine tasks. This is taken as evidence of a regression to passive dependency, and again the presence of anxiety is often inferred rather than measured, although many of these passive victims are also fearful.

Finally, the victims enter a "recovery stage" in which clinical manifestations of anxiety, apprehension, and tension appear, gradually subsiding as psychological equilibrium is regained. During this state nightmares are common, and victims characteristically feel a need to retell experiences repeatedly, often doing so with identical emphasis and detail each time. Such repeated telling of the traumatic events appears to be a form of desensitization, used by victims to reduce anxiety. Feelings of guilt about having failed to protect loved ones may become prominent during this stage, especially in cases where some measure of responsibility can be assigned. Depression over losses is also likely to follow.

Most psychological studies of civilian disaster focus on the recovery period, beginning hours or days after impact, and lasting typically for days or weeks. The large majority of victims appear to regain their psychological equilibrium within this time. However, precise data are unavailable, and long-range followup studies are rare. Because most of the available studies tend to be short term (four to six weeks), the presence, causes, and course of more enduring anxiety syndromes are not typically reported. However, in the few available long-term studies of civilian disaster, we find clear and convincing evidence of lasting anxiety in the form of chronic or delayed posttraumatic stress disorders (or traumatic neuroses). For example, in a 3 1/2 to 4 1/2 year followup of an explosion and fire aboard a gasoline tanker, Leopold and Dillon reported enduring, situationally specific anxiety, tension, and fearfulness in all survivors (15). In one-third of the survivors, these symptoms were so severe that they were unable to return to sea.

It might be appropriate here to anticipate several factors that future research may find particularly important in the causation or manifestation of anxiety in the aftermath of civilian disasters. Three such factors are impact characteristics, perceived human agency, and social isolation.

1. Impact characteristics may be defined in terms of two orthogonal dimensions: *spatial* and *temporal*. The *spatial* dimension refers to the "area" of an individual's life directly affected by the disaster. At one end of the range are disasters affecting relatively isolated and circumscribed areas—the survivor of a restaurant fire or an airline crash may still have his or her home, family, and livelihood intact, waiting to resume former roles. At the other end of the range are disasters affecting broad segments of life. Floods or hurricanes often deprive the survivor of family, home, employment, and community structure. The survivor may be forced to assume a number of unaccustomed and often difficult coping roles during a long aftermath. The *temporal* dimension refers to the length of time the individual is directly and

overtly exposed to the disaster, ranging from seconds or minutes in the case of a survivor who walks away from a traumatic vehicle accident, to months or years in the case of a flood survivor who has lost everything. Generally we expect that the amount of anxiety aroused by the trauma of civilian disaster will be proportional to both the area and duration of impact, and that the frequency and severity of posttraumatic stress disorder will also vary accordingly.

2. The factor of perceived human agency often plays a particularly important role in posttraumatic anxiety. Civilian disasters may be roughly rank ordered along a dimension of *attribution*. At one end of the range are disasters in which human agency appears to be minimal or nonexistent. Hurricanes, blizzards, earthquakes, and the like are commonly referred to as "natural disasters" or acts of God. Indeed, the very term disaster ("bad star") implies unavoidable cosmic ordination, or fate. At the other end of the range are traumata stemming from perceived human malevolence such as terrorist activities, rape, physical assault, police brutality, torture, etc. In the middle of the range are those traumata engendered by the joint operation of man and nature combined. The Irish potato famine is a famous historical example, and the Buffalo Creek Dam disaster is a more recent addition. It seems likely that the greater the role of human agency (maximal in the case of the torture victim) the greater will be the aftermath of anxiety, and the greater the intensity, extent, and duration of symptomatology in relation to the actual duration and severity of the trauma itself.

3. Social isolation represents a significant factor in the genesis of posttraumatic anxiety, not only because isolation itself can be frightening and stressful, but also because it represents the absence of one of the most important mitigating influences against the harmful effects of stress (i.e., the interpersonal support network of the individual). There is enormous healing power in the influence of a person's family, friends, and various trusted helpers such as ministers, physicians, and other significant supportive figures in his or her life situation.

Isolation from this network deprives the victim of an immensely helpful psychosocial resource in his effort to cope with the stress of trauma. In fact, such isolation in itself may be significantly traumatic; and isolation of prisoners may be used as a form of torture, or as a contributing factor to a total torture situation (58).

Military Trauma

Psychological trauma arising from military combat is the subject of an extensive literature, reflecting more than a century of serious thought. In war, large groups of young men are exposed to a range of traumatogenic agents. Individual backgrounds, including previous psychological adjustment and medical information, are available for scrutiny. Standardized treatments and followups are routinely instituted on a scale unheard of in civilian life.

On the other hand, the study of traumatic anxiety related to combat has several serious drawbacks. The traumata, even though they are episodic, tend to be repetitive, and cumulative effects (both negative and positive) hamper interpretations. Chronic physical factors also become a serious problem. Even without regard to enemy action, military combat is notoriously destructive to health. The soldier may be poorly nourished, severely fatigued, chronically sleep deprived, forced to live under primitive conditions in the field, and subject to low-level physical diseases, infections, infestations, and wounds. If he is taken prisoner all of these factors may become worse, and further complicated by abuse, deliberate neglect, or torture. The combined impact of such various traumata may be greater than the sum of the parts. Studies of such patients are necessarily difficult and extremely complicated. Nevertheless, a considerable body of useful data has been gathered.

Combat Exhaustion

Since the most recent mass exposure of U.S. citizens to trauma was the Vietnam War, a large proportion of the PTSD cases now seen are veterans of that war, and a large proportion of these cases apparently served in the combat zone.

Many combat soldiers develop transient stress reactions in the form of heightened startle responses and nightmares, or dissociative symptoms such as depersonalization or emotional numbing, but do not appear to develop massive anxiety. Such transient symptoms may remit spontaneously (decreasing in both frequency and intensity with time), and specific treatment generally is not required (16). The persistence of more chronic reactions accompanied by evidence of severe anxiety, and the well-publicized emergence of delayed PTSD in the postcombat era, have drawn much public and professional attention to war-related trauma and its lasting effects on otherwise healthy young men.

The clinical picture of combat exhaustion corresponds reasonably well with the DSM-III description of immediate (acute) PTSD. Although symptoms may vary somewhat with such factors as the branch of service, the nature and severity of trauma, the length of stress, and the personality of the victim, a surprising uniformity exists in the development of the clinical picture (14).

The first symptoms to appear include a decreasing ability to "maintain psychological integration" (i.e., keep an overall sense of proportion), irritability, and progressive sleep disturbances. Although desperately tired, the soldier is unable to fall asleep, or unable to stay asleep. Nightmares and night terrors become frequent visitors. The startle reaction, which becomes pronounced, generalizes to include even soft sounds, sudden movement, or light.

The triad of increased sensitivity (which might be termed "vigilance"), emotional irritability, and sleep disturbance, represents the incipient state of combat exhaustion and generally is recognized by the soldier himself. In World Wars I and II, characterized by long campaigns, frequent combat, and infrequent rest, this incipient state was observed to continue sometimes for periods of weeks or months (17). The delicacy of such an equilibrium was often shown by the capability of a single traumatic incident then to incapacitate the soldier.

The classical World War II picture of the soldier suffering

from combat exhaustion shows ravages of the soma, as well as the psyche. Menninger described such cases as dejected, dirty, depressed, weary, trembling, often tearful, sometimes confused and dissociated, and "unable to take any more" (18). Amnesia was not uncommon, and variably was interpreted as unconscious repression or conscious suppression. In Vietnam, soldiers were rarely exposed to prolonged shelling, and tended to be better fed and rested. As Coleman and co-workers pointed out, combat reactions seen in Vietnam tended to be more sudden and acute, in reaction to some particularly traumatic combat experience (14). These authors also noted that in most cases the overwhelming core of anxiety seen in combat exhaustion cases was not present to the same extent in physically wounded soldiers. Apparently the wound provided for some an "honorable" escape from the situation and removed the source of anxiety. This interpretation is strengthened by the observation that soldiers recovering from physical wounds and about to be returned to combat sometimes show delayed posttraumatic symptoms that were not present initially. Of course, the delayed reaction could have been forthcoming in any case.

PTSD and Vietnam Veterans

The delayed PTSD seen in Vietnam veterans may follow a symptom-free period lasting weeks, months, or even years. Presenting symptoms are much the same as those following major civilian disasters, and are dominated by psychological features (anxiety) rather than physical features (exhaustion) (16). Sleep disturbances (including nightmares or combat dreams) manifesting high anxiety levels seem to predominate; intrusive morbid or anxiety-laden thoughts are commonly reported during waking hours. A high level of vigilance may be reflected by hyperalertness and excessive startle. Irritability and explosively aggressive impulses are often reported, as are somewhat more vague (but no less troubling) feelings of detachment and estrangement.

While these symptoms are similar to the DSM-III criteria for PTSD, even a casual perusal of the literature reveals a plethora of syndromes and conditions described in Vietnam veterans. Terms such as "post-Vietnam syndrome" appear to cover a broad range of problems (or at least of symptom combinations) in addition to PTSD, rendering differential diagnosis problematic (16). The problem of differential diagnosis has become so severe that some mental health professionals have even questioned the nature of delayed PTSD in Vietnam veterans (19). It must be kept firmly in mind that many psychiatric problems, such as heroin addiction, came out of the Vietnam War. It has become common to hear of the "post-Vietnam syndrome," but Breen cogently questioned the specificity of the syndrome vis-á-vis the Vietnam War as opposed to any other war or major disaster (20). Many of the symptoms ascribed to the "post-Vietnam syndrome" by various authors are said to vary greatly from individual to individual and do not appear to be specific.

Van Putten and Emory argued that even in cases where symptoms of "traumatic war neuroses" (i.e., pre-1980 PTSD) are present they are frequently overlooked or misinterpreted: reduction in general level of functioning resembles the contraction of ego functioning found in schizophrenic deterioration; phobic elaborations about the world as an unbearably hostile place resembles persecutory delusion; explosive aggressivity and flashbacks to combat scenes have led to misdiagnoses of psychomotor epilepsy and LSD abuse (5).

The literature on posttraumatic reactions is further complicated by references to acute "psychoticlike states," "paranoid-aggressive states," "puzzling acute anxiety paranoia," "chronic psychosislike states," "chronic psychosislike pictures," "quasi-psychotic attacks," and "hallucinatory," "semihallucinatory," and even "quasi-hallucinatory" dissociative states, none of which is defined in terms allowing comparison across studies (21-24).

The Vietnam War left in its wake a wide range of psychological casualties. The numbers or even proportions of Vietnam veterans suffering from some approximation of PTSD is the subject of a correspondingly wide range of speculation. Bourne reported that only 5 percent of psychiatric admissions from Vietnam were diagnosed "combat fatigue" (as opposed to 40 percent diagnosed character and behavior disorder) (25). Strange studied Vietnam psychiatric evacuees on board a hospital ship, and concluded that "combat fatigue" was present in about 15 percent of his sample (26). Blank noted that most studies indicate that about 20 percent of Vietnam veterans have "substantial war-related psychological difficulties impairing their lives," but the proportion of PTSD is not clear (27). Frye and Stockton reported full-blown PTSD in 24 percent (and borderline symptoms in another 19 percent) of their sample of officer candidate school personnel who had served in Vietnam 10 years previously (28). Egendorf estimated that 20-30 percent of Vietnam veterans are diagnosable as suffering from PTSD, but that altogether 50 percent show signs of unresolved, troubling war experiences. Egendorf speculated that "subclinical malaise" may affect 2 million Vietnam veterans—a majority of those who served (29).

The Heuristic Approach to Treatment

In World War II it was found that evacuation and treatment of combat exhaustion casualties in rear area hospitals allowed less than 10 percent of the casualties to return to duty (18). Immediate short-term treatment within 15-20 miles of the battle zone, however, allowed about 60 percent to return to duty (and in most cases to maintain successful adjustment) (30). In Korea, 65-75 percent of the cases treated at or below divisional level (i.e., very close to the combat zone) were able to return to duty, and less than 10 percent of those had to be treated a second time (31).

In addition to its correlation with increasingly effective treatment, the heuristic emphasis on situational specificity allowed prophylactic measures to be developed. Soldiers increasingly came to be taught that fear and anxiety are normal concomitants of battle rather than signs of cowardice or symptoms of neurosis. Officers were taught to recognize the development of combat exhaustion symptoms and to bring soldiers to the nearest aid station for immediate treatment. As a result of these and other factors, the incidence of combat exhaustion cases evacuated to rear areas fell progressively from 10 percent in World War II (32) to 6 percent early in the Korean War (33) to less than 1.5 percent in Vietnam (25,34).

On the basis of practical lessons learned during the wars of this century, an effective treatment strategy for cases of acute combat exhaustion has emerged. It has been found that symptoms may quickly be reversed by removal from combat and provision of brief supportive psychotherapy, coupled with warm food and mild sedation. Three guiding principles may be discerned (14,35).

1. *Immediacy:* Officers are taught to watch for signs of incipient combat exhaustion or traumatic stress disorder, and to have the affected soldier taken immediately to the nearest aid station. Specially trained medics encourage the soldier to talk about recent traumatic events, and a hot meal coupled with mild sedation are used to ensure a good night's sleep. Typically the soldier is able to return to duty the following morning.

2. *Proximity:* Treatment takes place as near as possible to the combat unit, within the combat zone, because removal to an interior zone has been found to encourage maintenance of symptoms and a reluctance to return to the unit. Soldiers not responding to treatment at the nearest aid station are removed only as far as division level, where more intensive rest and supportive therapy are given. The soldier generally is able to return to his unit after 72 hours, but if still more intensive treatment is needed, he is evacuated to an interior zone hospital for treatment on a professionally staffed psychiatric ward.

3. *Expectancy:* A carefully planned duty-expectant attitude is maintained to convince the traumatized soldier that anxiety and fear are normal concomitants of battle, and that every soldier is expected to perform combat duties despite anxiety and traumatic experiences. An expectancy of prompt recovery and return to the unit is also maintained to prevent secondary gain from symptom maintenance. Psychiatric labels implying psychological failure are avoided.

Levan and co-workers suggested adding *brevity* to these three principles because their experience treating Israeli casualties from the 1973 Yom Kippur War indicated that the best results seem to be produced when treatment is not prolonged (36).

Other Treatments

To treat both acute and delayed combat stress, Grinker found narcosynthesis to be effective. Under heavy sedation a reexperiencing and abreaction of feelings (repressed and otherwise) allowed synthesis by the conscious ego (37). Although more contemporary approaches may also use pharmacological adjuncts (38), most rely on group therapy (39), and most appear to accept at least tacitly the contention that a debriefing from military experience, however belated, is important for recovery (40).

In all such cases, there seems to be a consensus that therapy should be oriented to reality factors to a greater degree than in the traditional treatment of neuroses. The trauma was real, and treatment must focus on symptoms resulting from the patient's reactions to stress. To this end, the patient is encouraged to vent feelings regarded as realistic under the circumstances, and to work through such feelings until he or she can be comfortable with them (16).

Learning Theory Concepts

Within the context of learning theory, the question has arisen as to how the concept of anxiety, or even fear (being a central motivational state not directly observable) can be defined objectively (41). The answer, at least in part, has been to define anxiety in terms of its antecedent conditions—using a classical conditioning paradigm employing a traumatic stimulus.

The sequence of a neutral "warning stimulus" (CS) followed by traumatic stimulus (UCS) operationally defines a state of anxiety intervening between the two (42). By the process of classical conditioning, the warning (CS) comes to elicit responses originally elicited only by the traumatic UCS. For our purposes, the most important of these responses is the central motivational state of fear (anxiety). The motivational state, of course, is not directly observable, but is studied through changes in other measurable behaviors such as galvanic skin response or heart rate, which are taken as indices of anxiety (43).

Fear has two important characteristics: it "energizes" behavior and its reduction is reinforcing. The energizing characteristic was neatly demonstrated by Brown and co-workers who showed that the presentation of a warning CS that previously had been associated with electric shock (and which therefore should arouse anxiety) greatly increased the magnitude of a startle response elicited by an unexpected pistol shot. The reinforcing characteristic of anxiety reduction is shown by the general finding that responses that terminate or otherwise allow escape from the warning CS (thereby reducing anxiety) are quickly learned and tend to resist extinction. This phenomenon has been the subject of extensive and thorough study from the viewpoints of learning theory and motivational theory, and has profound implications for the treatment of pathological behavior (44,45).

Applications of the conditioning model to PTSD are many and pervasive. Combat has all of the elements necessary for the conditioning of anxiety. Warning CSs are numerous and varied; the very real threat of death and injury is a potent UCS arousing fear and anxiety. The classical conditioning process involves association of these warning CSs with the central motivational state of fear/anxiety aroused by the UCS.

In addition, the training received by a soldier is a conditioning experience, instrumental conditioning in this case, of specific combat behaviors. Because in combat ordinary methods of coping are relatively useless, these new instrumental behaviors (returning fire, for example) serve to remove the external threat and reduce anxiety. In this manner anxiety arousal by a warning CS serves to energize and motivate an instrumental response leading to reinforcement through anxiety reduction.

Conflict arises when other, incompatible response tendencies (e.g., flight or freezing) are aroused simultaneously with the desired instrumental response. In such a situation the warning CS (and the danger itself) is not reduced, and anxiety is compounded. In the laboratory, conflict has been used for more than half a century to produce "experimental neurosis" in animals. Its symptoms are startingly similar to those seen in human "combat neurosis": sympathetic arousal, trembling, lacrimation, catatoniclike reactions, or "freezing,"and so on (46).

Following such a single traumatic incident the soldier (like the experimental laboratory animal) is likely to show signs indicative of continuing high anxiety levels (galvanic skin response, heart rate, startle). The soldier is also likely, with time, to acquire one or several pathological (or instrumental) responses that serve to reduce anxiety (displacement behaviors, repression, suppression, regression, and denial behaviors). In severe cases, the pathological symptoms may spread to include several types of behavior and several different organ systems following even a single traumatic incident.

By the two-factor model relating classical and instrumental conditioning, the trauma of combat (UCS) arouses anxiety (CR), which becomes classically conditioned to the environmental cues (CS) present at the time. To reduce anxiety (i.e., to eliminate or escape from an anxiety-arousing CS), appropriate instrumental behaviors (returning fire, assault) may be performed. Inappropriate conflicting behavior tendencies (freezing, flight), which either fail to reduce anxiety-arousing CSs (freezing) or which reduce them temporarily but lead to greater problems in the future (flight), may also be aroused. In cases where appropriate responses are not performed, anxiety may be compounded, leading to autonomic signs of dysfunction and to the acquisition of sundry neurotic instrumental behaviors, which reduce anxiety in a more problematic manner.

Appropriate instrumental behaviors in a combat environment are not, of course, limited to returning fire and assaults, but include the entire repertory of behaviors that allow anxiety to be controlled in a militarily and personally acceptable manner. In Vietnam, the primary or even exclusive motivating force was survival, and psychological defense mechanisms such as denial, psychic numbing, and repression helped soldiers to cope with extreme combat conditions, uncertainty, and the unpredictability of jungle warfare. As the level of combat increased so did the intensity of these defense mechanisms (28). They facilitated survival by reducing anxiety and thus were adaptive in combat, but paradoxically these defenses set the stage for PTSD later in civilian life.

If anxiety reduction in combat involves the performance of certain instrumental behaviors serving to reduce anxiety-evoking warning CSs, then personnel who do not have these combat responses in their behavioral repertories might be expected to suffer high levels of PTSD. This appears to have been the case during Israel's Yom Kippur War; personnel in direct support units suffered a disproportionately high rate of psychiatric casualties as compared to personnel in combat units. When subjected to enemy fire, support personnel had no means of counter-assaulting, returning fire, or otherwise responding to the threat in an acceptable manner. Officers were shown to be less vulnerable to psychiatric debilitation in combat than were enlisted men, perhaps in part because the former had available a wider range of appropriate responses from which to choose. Adaptation to anxiety through direct combat activity seems to diminish psychiatric risk (36). Hendin and co-workers cited studies of physiological stress indicators and their own experience with Vietnam combat veterans to show that the response to the stress of combat is not necessarily a function of the intensity or duration of the experience, but that it depends on the meaning of the experience to the individual and the protective or adaptive mechanisms used to cope with it (47).

The often-noted tendency of PTSDs to become chronic in the absence of treatment is entirely in accord with laboratory studies of classically conditioned anxiety. For example, in a landmark study by Solomon and co-workers, dogs were trained to avoid a traumatic electric shock by jumping a hurdle into a safe compartment. A warning CS predicted imminent shock onset, and the criterion for acquisition was the performance of ten successive avoidance responses. Following acquisition, extinction was instituted by turning the shock off, and exposing animals to the warning CS only. In 200 extinction trials, no animal failed to respond to the CS, and at the end of extinction the mean response latency was even shorter than at the end of acquisition (48). This extreme resistance to extinction of classically conditioned anxiety is characteristic of studies employing very intense (i.e., traumatic) aversive UCSs. In PTSD victims, the continuing high levels of anxiety elicited by internal and environmental CSs are often manifested by hyperalertness, exaggerated startle, sleep disturbances, memory impairment, trouble concentrating, and other symptoms of autonomic dysfunction.

In addition to the resistance to extinction of instrumental behaviors reinforced by anxiety reduction, the autonomic signs of anxiety are similarly resistant. Autonomic signs of "experimental neurosis" have persisted for almost four years after conditioning in sheep (49) and for up to ten years in dogs (46).

In humans, instrumentally conditioned combat responses originally acquired to reduce anxiety may be cognitively inhibited after return to a civilian environment. This does not, however, imply that the classically conditioned anxiety has been extinguished. Edwards and Acker recorded GSRs from a group of Navy veterans who had seen sea duty during World War II (50). When compared to a group of Army World War II veterans, the Navy men showed dramatically increased GSRs when exposed to the sound of the Navy "general quarters" (battle stations) gong. The elicitation of this classically conditioned autonomic response 15-20 years after conditioning implies that anxiety may persist even in the absence of anxiety-motivated instrumental behavior—a phenomenon called schizokinesis by Gantt (51).

In a similar study more directly addressing anxiety (in addition to its autonomic signs), Dobbs and Wilson compared three groups of men: a control group who had not had combat experience; a group of "compensated" combat veterans showing satisfactory social adjustment, regular work habits, and no signs of psychiatric disability; and a group of "decompensated" combat veterans, composed of (nonpsychotic) VA patients whose psychiatric symptoms dated from the time of their combat experience, who had unsatisfactory work adjustment, and who showed psychiatric symptoms typical of combat neurosis (52). Electroencephalogram (EEG), electrocardiogram (EKG), and respiration were recorded as subjects listened to an eight-minute tape of combat sounds (artillery barage, small arms, and aerial bombardment, with strobe flashes synchronized with explosions for the second four minutes).

After listening to the tape the subjects were interviewed to determine their subjective reactions.

The *noncombat control* group showed responses to the tape indicative of a brief orienting response (initial transient increase in attention, pulse, and respiration) followed by inattention, and sometimes even drowsiness and sleep. The *compensated group of combat veterans* showed mild to marked physiological (heart rate and respiration) and behavioral (motor) responses that were considered to be classically conditioned responses resulting from combat experience; 69 percent showed obvious signs of anxiety, and one demanded that the experiment be stopped because of the severity of anxiety aroused. Several commented on noticeable autonomic responses in addition to those measured (sweating, dryness of mouth, lacrimation), feelings of helplessness, wanting to take cover or run. Noticeable motor responses consisted of clasping of the hands, and marked startle (recorded as EEG artifact) to the light flashes. The *decompensated group of combat veterans* showed markedly disturbed behavioral responses so severe that physiological recording was impossible; 63 percent terminated the experiment after listening to the tape for periods of a few seconds to four minutes (when the flashes began). Decompensated subjects demonstrated severe anxiety with restlessness, purposeless movement of the extremities, thrashing, and escape. At times their behavior was deemed nearly psychotic, and neurotic symptoms were intensified for varying periods after the experiment. Marked sweating was noted and dryness of the mouth reported. By the end of the experiment all subjects in this decompensated group of combat veterans appeared extremely anxious. Some were tremulous, some tearful, three developed speech difficulties (stammer), and one became almost inarticulate. Remarkably, all of these symptoms were elicited many years after combat.

Delayed PTSD

A problem that has gained much recent attention is the delayed form of PTSD—specifically, the appearance of symptoms of post-Vietnam combat stress in the civilian environment after a symptom-free interval spanning months or years. Similar phenomena have been reported in a significant proportion of the 700,000 or so concentration camp survivors of World War II. These cases may be explained on the basis of the conditioning model as follows.

At the end of a tour of combat duty, or following release from confinement, the soldier makes an often precipitous transition into a new stimulus environment, more or less free from the specific anxiety-arousing warning-type CSs characteristic of the old environment. With precipitous transition, discrimination between the old and new environments is easily made—the two are seen to have many differences and few similarities. Instrumental behaviors learned in the old environment to handle anxiety are not elicited as frequently in the new environment for several reasons. The absence of specific anxiety-arousing CSs means lower anxiety levels and lower anxiety drive; the instrumental responses themselves may not transfer completely to the new stimulus environment (generalization decrement); and the expression of the instrumental responses may be cognitively inhibited or suppressed as socially or otherwise inappropriate. These factors may underlie the symptom-free interval. As time passes, however, pathological (i.e., situationally inappropriate) behavior may reemerge. This evidently reflects the conditioning of anxiety not only to specific warning CSs, but also to more ubiquitous environmental cues, a phenomenon described in some detail in laboratory animals (43). Such conditioning has been shown to occur in humans without conscious awareness, and autonomic responses can be conditioned to symbolic, as well as to concrete stimuli (53).

Although conditioning to secondary stimuli may initially be too weak to arouse anxiety in the new environment, the amount of stimulus generalization increases with time (43), and there appears to be a residual effect of the original anxiety conditioning that transfers to the new environment (54). Through increasing stimulus generalization over time, classically conditioned anxiety may be rearoused by secondary, seemingly innocuous, stimuli in the new environment, producing the symptoms of delayed PTSD.

Previously successful methods of dealing with aroused anxiety (instrumental combat responses) are generally seen as inappropriate in a civilian environment. On occasion, however, these responses may be aroused, even appearing as episodes of explosive aggression against seemingly innocent people or objects (55).

The problem of delayed PTSDs arising from combat may grow increasingly frequent as World War II, Korean, and Vietnam veterans age. A 20-year follow-up study of World War II veterans conducted by Archibald and Tuddenham found an increasing incidence of new patients seeking psychiatric care for war neuroses. Traumatic stress symptoms, latent since World War II, became evident during the aging process, triggered by previously innocuous environmental events simulating the original trauma. The authors suggest that the vicissitudes of aging (parental loss, children leaving home, retirement, increasing medical disabilities) all serve as stressors that may reactivate the latent traumatic stress disorder (56).

The point has been made previously that instrumental avoidance responses adopted by animals to reduce classically conditioned anxiety are extremely resistant to extinction. We have also noted that many of the symptoms of PTSD appear to be lingering avoidance responses (e.g., psychic numbing, avoidance of activities and situations reminiscent of combat) or the autonomic signs of anxiety itself (e.g., startle, sleep disturbances). Because the symptoms of delayed or chronic PTSD do not spontaneously improve with time, but become increasingly refractory to treatment, it is important that effective treatment be instituted as soon as the disorder is recognized (57). Laboratory studies of conditioning suggest several effective treatment strategies.

One strategy involves the forced exposure of the subject to the anxiety-arousing CSs in the original conditioning. Solomon and co-workers locked their experimental dogs in the chamber where traumatic shocks had originally been experienced, thereby preventing the instrumental avoidance response and forcing CS exposure in the absence of shock (48). Returning the traumatized soldier to combat exposes him again to anxiety-arousing CSs of battle without (it is hoped) the overwhelming anxiety elicited by the original trauma. The soldier is then able to use militarily appropriate instrumental behaviors to control the "normal" combat anxiety in accordance with his training.

In most cases, return to the original anxiety-conditioning environment is impractical, and we must rely on the reconstruction of similar situations within which anxiety extinction can occur and from which extinction may generalize. In the laboratory, of course, we can literally reconstruct situations similar to those of initial conditioning, manipulating discrete cues, and empirically assessing the importance of various environmental and subject factors. Outside the laboratory, in the "real world" of anxiety-ridden humans, the most common sort of reconstructions occur spontaneously in the form of intrusive thoughts and dreams. Long viewed as belated attempts to master the overwhelming anxiety arising from the original traumatic situation, these informal, spontaneous reconstructions, like their more formal, therapist-guided counterparts, may also be seen within the context of conditioning theory as self-imposed extinction trials. The beneficial effects of emotionally cathartic reconstructions of traumatic experiences in both individual and group psychotherapy are well known, and should be employed without delay when PTSD is diagnosed.

Prisoner Trauma

The posttraumatic anxiety of prisoners depends largely on the circumstances of imprisonment. Western penal institutions, while far from pleasant, are a far cry from POW camps or modern interrogation centers where torture is employed. The horror of Nazi concentration/extermination camps still defies adequate description.

In POW and concentration camps the trauma was prolonged, and often extreme. Victims were poorly nourished at best, and starvation was common. However, the severest elements of trauma, and those resulting in the most profound posttraumatic anxiety states, were those involving deliberate cruelty, brutalization, and torture of prisoners. The effectiveness of such treatment in producing compliant behavior in prisoners through terror, debility, and dependency, has been described (58).

Torture in all its implications may well be the most powerful generator of PTSD in human experience. In the experience of health professionals in those countries fortunate enough to be relatively free of this dreadful practice, the closest thing to the torture victim is the battered child. The frequency of PTSD in brutalized children is probably far higher than has been reported up to the present, and offers a most important prospect for further clinical research on posttraumatic anxiety.

References

1. Farber IE, West LJ: Conceptual problems of research on emotions. Psychiatr 12:1-7, 1960

2. Freedman AM, Kaplan HI: Comprehensive Textbook of Psychiatry. Baltimore, Williams and Wilkins, p 1022, 1967

3. American Psychiatric Association: Diagnostic and Statistical Manual of Mental Disorders, 3rd ed. Washington, DC, American Psychiatric Association, 1980

4. American Psychiatric Association: Diagnostic and Statistical Manual of Mental Disorders, 2nd ed. Washington, DC, American Psychiatric Association, 1968

5. Van Putten T, Emory WH: Traumatic neurosis in Vietnam returnees. Arch Gen Psychiatry 29:695-698, 1973

6. Bozzuto JC: Cinematic neurosis following "The Exorcist." Report of four cases. J Nerv Ment Dis 161:43-48, 1975

7. Horowitz MJ, Solomon GF: Delayed stress response in Vietnam veterans, in Stress Disorders Among Viet-

nam Veterans: Theory, Research, and Treatment. Edited by Figley CR. New York, Brunner/Mazel, pp 84-96, 1978

8. White GF, Haas JE: Assessment of Research on Natural Hazards. Cambridge, MA, MIT Press, 1975

9. Fredrick CJ: Violence and disasters; immediate and long-term consequences. Submitted for publication at the request of the World Health Organization, 1981. (Paper presented to working group conference on the psychological consequences of violence, The Hague, April 6-10, 1981)

10. Glass AJ: Psychological aspects of disaster. JAMA 171:222-227, 1959

11. Popovic M, Petrovic D: After the earthquake. Lancet 3707:1169-1171, 1964

12. Zusman J: Meeting mental health needs in a disaster, in Emergency and Disaster Management. Edited by Parad HJ, Resnik HP, Parad LG. Bowie, MD, The Charles Press, 1976

13. Melick ME, Logue JN, Fredrick CJ: Stress and disaster, in Handbook of Stress. Edited by Melick M. New York, Free Press, pp 613-630, 1982

14. Coleman JC, Butcher JN, Carson RC: Abnormal Psychology and Modern Life. Glenview, Ill: Scott, Foresman, pp 171-203, 1980

15. Leopold RL, Dillon H: Psychoanatomy of a disaster: a long-term study of posttraumatic neurosis in survivors of a marine explosion. Am J Psychiatry 119:913-921, 1963

16. Ewalt JR, Crawford D: Posttraumatic stress syndrome. Current Psychiatr Ther 38:145-153, 1981

17. Bartemeier LH, Kube LS, Menninger KA, et al: Combat exhaustion. J Nerv Ment Dis 104:385-525, 1946

18. Menninger WC: Psychiatry in a Troubled World. New York, Macmillan, 1948

19. Lipkin JO, Blank AS, Parson ER, Smith J: Vietnam veterans and posttraumatic stress disorder. Hosp Community Psychiatry 33:908-912, 1982

20. Breen HJ: Post Vietnam syndrome: a critique. Arizona Medicine 39:791-793, 1982

21. Grinker RR, Spiegel JP: Men Under Stress. New York, McGraw-Hill, 1963

22. Tausk V: Diagnostic considerations concerning the symptomatology of the so-called war psychoses. Psychoanal Quart 38:382-405, 1969

23. Niederland WG: Clinical observations on the "survivor syndrome." Int J Psychoanal 49:313-315, 1968

24. Jaffe R: Dissociative phenomena in former concentration camp inmates. Int J Psychoanal 49:310-312, 1968

25. Bourne PG: Military psychiatry and the Vietnam experience. Am J Psychiatry 127:481-488, 1970

26. Strange RE: Effects of combat stress on hospital ship psychiatric evacuees, in Psychology and Physiology of Stress. Edited by Bourne PG. New York, Academic Press, pp 75-83, 1969

27. Blank AS: Apocalypse terminable and interminable: operation outreach for Vietnam veterans. Hosp Community Psychiatry 33:913-918, 1982

28. Frye JS, Stockton RA: Discriminant analysis of posttraumatic stress disorder among a group of Vietnam veterans. Am J Psychiatry 139:52-56, 1982

29. Egendorf A: The postwar healing of Vietnam veterans: recent research. Hosp Community Psychiatry 33:901-908, 1982

30. Ludwig AO, Ranson SW: A statistical follow-up of treatment of combat-induced psychiatric casualties, I and II. Military Surgeon 100:51-62, 169-175, 1947

31. Hausman W, Rioch DM: Military psychiatry. Arch Gen Psychiatry 16:727-739, 1967

32. Bloch HS: Army clinical psychiatry in the combat zone—1967-1968. Am J Psychiatry 126:289-298, 1969

33. Bell E Jr: The basis of effective military psychiatry. Dis Nerv Sys 19:283-288, 1958

34. Allerton WS: Psychiatric casualties in Vietnam. Roche Medical Image and Commentary 12:27, 1970

35. Artiss KL: Human behavior under stress—from combat to social psychiatry. Milit Med 128:1011-1015, 1963

36. Levan I, Greenfeld H, Baruch E: Psychiatric combat reactions during the Yom Kippur War. Am J Psychiatry 136:637-641, 1979

37. Grinker RR: Psychiatric disorders in combat crews overseas and returnees. Med Clin North Am 29:729-739, 1945

38. Walker JI: Chemotherapy of traumatic war stress. Milit Med 147:1029-1033, 1982

39. Christenson RM, Walker JI, Ross DR, Maltbie AA: Reaction of traumatic conflicts. Am J Psychiatry 138:984-985, 1982

40. Berman S, Gusman F: An inpatient program for Vietnam combat veterans in a Veterans Administration hospital. Hosp Community Psychiatry 33:919-922, 1982

41. Solomon RL, Brush ES: Experimentally derived conceptions of anxiety and aversion, in Nebraska Symposium on Motivation. Edited by Jones MR. Lincoln, NE, Univ of Nebraska Press, pp 212-305, 1956

42. Zeaman D, Smith RW: Review of some recent findings in human cardiac conditioning, in Classical Conditioning: A Symposium. Edited by Prokasy WF. New York, Appleton-Century-Crofts, pp 378-418, 1965

43. McAllister WR, McAllister DE: Variables influencing the conditioning and the measurement of acquired

fear, in Classical Conditioning: A Symposium. Edited by Prokasy WF. New York, Appleton-Century-Crofts, pp 172-191, 1965

44. Mackintosh NJ: The Psychology of Animal Learning. New York, Academic Press, 1974

45. Cofer CN, Appley MH: Motivation: Theory and Research. New York, John Wiley & Sons, 1964

46. Gantt WH: The Experimental Basis for Neurotic Behavior. New York, Hoeber, 1944

47. Hendin H, Pollinger A, Singer P, Ulman RB: Meanings of combat and the development of posttraumatic stress disorder. Am J Psychiatry 138:1490-1493, 1981

48. Solomon RL, Kamin LJ, Wynne LC: Traumatic avoidance learning: the outcomes of several extinction procedures with dogs. J Abnorm Social Psychol 48:291-302, 1953

49. Anderson OD, Paramenter R: A long-term study of the Experimental neurosis in the sheep and dog. Psychosom Med Monog 2:1-150, 1941

50. Edwards AE, Acker LE: A demonstration of the long-term retention of a conditioned GSR. Psychosom Med 24:459-463, 1962

51. Gantt WH: The physiological basis of psychiatry: the conditioned reflex, in Basic Problems in Psychiatry. Edited by Wortis J. New York, Grune & Stratton, pp 778-798, 1953

52. Dobbs D, Wilson WP: Observations on persistence of war neurosis. Dis Nerv Sys 21:686-691, 1960

53. Grings WW: Verbal-perceptual factors in the conditioning of autonomic responses, in Classical Conditioning: A Symposium. Edited by Prokasy WF. New York, Appleton-Century-Crofts, pp 71-89, 1965

54. Scheflen NA: Generalization and extinction of experimentally induced fear in cats, in Experimental Psycho-

pathology. Edited by Hock PH, Zubin J. New York, Grune & Stratton, pp 1-11, 1957

55. Shatan: Stress disorders among Vietnam veterans: the emotional content of combat continues, in Stress Disorders Among Vietnam Veterans: Theory, Research and Treatment. Edited by Figley GR. New York, Brunner/Mazel, pp 56-83, 1978

56. Archibald HC, Tuddenham RD: Persistent stress reaction after combat. Arch Gen Psychiatry 12:475-481, 1965

57. Cavenar JO, Nash JL: The effects of combat on the normal personality: war neurosis in Vietnam returnees. Compr Psychiatry 17:647-653, 1976

58. Farber IE, Harlow HF, West LJ: Brainwashing, conditioning and DDD (debility, dependency, and dread). Sociometry 20:271-285, 1957

5

The Psychodynamic View of Anxiety

John C. Nemiah, M.D.

5

The Psychodynamic View of Anxiety

John C. Nemiah, M.D.

The Psychoanalytic Process

Any discussion of the psychodynamic approach to the treatment of anxiety must be based on an understanding of the nature of anxiety itself and its role in psychological conflict and symptom formation. This chapter begins, therefore, with a brief synopsis of the psychoanalytic view of anxiety. In its turn, this view provides the conceptual framework for the clinical evaluation designed to determine the criteria for the application of psychoanalytically oriented psychotherapy to patients suffering from anxiety disorders.

In classical psychoanalytic theory, anxiety is viewed as an ego affect that is at the same time a central indicator of psychological conflict. The presence or emergence of anxiety during the clinical interview serves as a guide to areas of conflict that need exploration and resolution by psychoanalytic techniques. In the course of the patient's free associations, therefore, attention is initially directed to those associations which arouse anxiety. Detecting and analyzing the defenses to facilitate the emergence of previously unconscious mental elements is the next step. These, in turn, give an increasingly clear indication of the underlying nucleus of the conflict and determine the ultimate use of an interpretation, which delivers the pathogenic nucleus itself into the light of consciousness. The result is that the patient achieves insight, an expansion of consciousness, the resolution of the conflict, and the disappearance of symptoms.

This brief summary has, of course, tremendously telescoped and oversimplified the nature of the analytic process. Nothing has been said about the need for "working through," which characterizes most courses of treatment—that is, the need repeatedly to analyze the defenses, to make interpretations, and to help the patient to ever-increasing insight before the final resolution of the conflict can take place. Furthermore, it is necessary to help the patient constantly to make connections between his present dynamic conflicts and earlier genetic childhood conflicts, as well as between these elements and their manifestation in the transference. In most psychoanalytic therapies there is an equal distribution of therapeutic attention to all three of these phenomena (past, present, and transference relationships); in classical psychoanalysis the nurturing and subsequent analysis of the transference itself holds the center of the stage.

Nature of Anxiety and the Course of Treatment

Such an oversimplification runs the risk of trivializing the nature of the analytic process by reducing it to an almost meaningless formula. Let us, therefore, examine a course of treatment as it actually occurred in a patient, not only to put flesh on the naked skeleton of abstractions, but also to provide clinical observations as a basis for the later discussion of the nature of anxiety. By modern standards the treatment hardly qualifies for the designation of psychoanalysis proper—though it has certain affinities with some of the earliest psychoanalytic cathartic procedures de-

scribed in Breuer and Freud's *Studies on Hysteria* (1).
Although the therapeutic result was quite satisfactory, the
actual treatment lasted for only three sessions. Furthermore, the patient had two therapists, a medical student and
his supervisor, each of whom saw her once alone, and then
together for a third and final session.

The patient, a married woman of 25, was admitted to the
psychiatric ward for typical symptoms of anxiety that had
become so severe and disabling that she was unable to
carry on at home. The illness had first appeared two
months before admission. She had then experienced the
sudden outbreak of anxiety attacks in association with
distressing "obscene thoughts." These consisted of a recurrent mental image of herself and her father, both naked,
engaged in sexual activity. To control the associated anxiety the patient attempted to push the images out of her
mind by shaking her head vigorously and forcing herself to
think about other things. Despite this the obscene images
forced themselves on her attention with a power of their
own. She described them as follows: "They were just
thoughts about sex. Sometimes I would ask him [her fa-
ther], and sometimes he would ask me. I could see pictures
of him in my mind—you know, with no clothes."

During her first two weeks in the hospital there was no
basic change in the patient's condition. She was somewhat
relieved to be hospitalized, but the images and anxiety
continued to plague her without surcease. Despite regular
exploratory interviews with a resident physician, no significant progress had been made in understanding or removing
her symptoms. At the end of this initial two-week evaluation the patient was first seen by the medical student's
supervisor. The patient began the interview by describing
her anxiety and the images that relentlessly beleaguered
her. The content of these images was not only distressing to
the patient but surprised her as well, for she had always
found her father a difficult, disagreeable man and could
never remember a time when she had liked him. Indeed,
she had always tried to keep out of his way and to avoid
talking to him when she was forced to be with him. In the
course of describing her symptoms she revealed that they
had first occurred at the end of a period of a week when her

father had been trying to make friendly, helpful overtures to her during a minor financial difficulty that she and her husband experienced. She described her relationship with her father as follows:*

> PT: My father was mean to me when I was little. I hate my father. [He] was never good to me. He wouldn't even speak to me. Or, if he did, it would be very mean and sarcastic. He'd swear at me. He would say that he didn't want me. He just never wanted me around. I sort of feel as though I missed something.
>
> DR: Missed what?
>
> PT: Well, like when little girls—you know, when their fathers—sometimes they pick them up or fool with them, or even just maybe say something pleasant to them.
>
> DR: That never happened to you?
>
> PT: Never. I mean I don't ever remember it. My mother said when I was little, my father wasn't mean, but I don't remember when. Since I can remember, he wouldn't speak to me or anything. My mother said he was good to me, and he used to sing songs to me, to take me on his lap, but I don't remember. I don't ever remember when he was good to me. I only remember when he was mean to me. That's all I remember.

A bit later, in talking about how her father had tried to be nice to her during the week before her symptoms began, she said:

> PT: I think maybe my mother told my father not to be so mean to me, because he said a few things in a sort of nice way—not really nice, but not like him. I didn't know what to do or say. I was sort of confused.
>
> DR: Are you afraid when he is nice to you?
>
> PT: Well, I'm not—I don't know what to say. He's not nice to me, really, very often. I'd like to be nice to him, but I'm sort of afraid to. I just am glad when he keeps on talking to me mean the way he always does.
>
> DR: You mean?
>
> PT: He'd yell at me. I sort of know and expect that—I'm used to that. That's all I know about my father. I just wouldn't know what to do if he was nice to me.
>
> DR: Do you want him to be nice to you?
>
> PT: No, I don't.

---

* Indented quotations are taken verbatim from transcriptions of taped interviews.

DR: Was there a time when you wanted him to be nice to you?

PT: When I was little, I just wanted him to—maybe sometimes pick me up and talk to me about something—that's all. I wanted just to know that he did love me a little bit. I guess I always wanted him to be nice to me, but when I stop to think about him, I guess I didn't want him to be nice to me.

DR: It sounds as though a part of you wants to be close to your father?

PT: (Here the patient begins sobbing.) I don't know how to be close to my father. I am too old to care about my father now.

Two things become apparent from what the patient says. First, behind her dislike for her father is a strong feeling of need and love for him. Second, she is at the same time afraid of these feelings and is more comfortable when the relationship is a distant and angry one. Motivated by her fear of closeness, she has defensively kept her distance from her father during her adult life to avoid the underlying frightening longing for a warm, loving relationship with him. In addition, she has erected the defense of reaction-formation in her emphasis on her hatred of her father, which enables her to exclude from awareness her loving wishes.

As these defenses were being explored in the interview, the patient recovered a memory of an event that had not been consciously available to her since it had happened nearly 15 years before: At age 11, and while in the living room with her father, she had had the sudden image of her father and herself together naked in a sexual embrace; terrified, she had run into the kitchen to find shelter with her mother. The frightening thought had not recurred, and she had forgotten about it until the memory emerged in the interview. With this new bit of history it became apparent that there had been an earlier, transient outbreak of the same symptom that now formed the central feature of her adult illness.

As the patient recalled and reported this long-lost memory she became intensely anxious, spoke more and more haltingly in a barely audible whisper, lowered her head into her lap (thus hiding her face from the interviewer), covered her ears with her hands as if she were trying to shut out some sound, and finally stopped talking altogether. At that point the doctor asked her, "What are you thinking right now?"

PT: My father.
DR: Yes, what about him? It's important.
PT: (Breaking into violent sobs.) With his clothes off.
DR: Why do you cover up your ears? Can you hear some-
    thing?
PT: No, I don't hear anything—it helps me to stop thinking.
DR: Did you hear something at some time?
PT: No, I never heard anything.
DR: You don't think that by accident you ever walked in on
    your parents when they were having relations, do you?

This highly leading question was in essence an interpretation; that is, an intervention by the doctor aimed at what he hypothesized was the unconscious content behind the surface behavior he was observing. The hypothesis itself was based on three considerations:

1. The marked anxiety and shame experienced by the patient indicated that the surface content was close to the underlying source of psychological conflict;
2. The peculiar behavior of the patient, who looked as if she were trying to stop up her ears against sound;
3. The theoretical knowledge, derived from observation of other patients, that the witnessing of parental intercourse as a child, especially during the oedipal phase (the "primal scene"), can leave behind unconscious anxiety-provoking memories and developmental fixations.

These mental processes of the interviewer actually occupied far less time than it has taken to describe them here. During the interview itself they were condensed into an intuitive flash that led to the doctor's question. The patient's response was interesting. She did not answer the question directly but replied by providing information that had not been obtained from her during any previous interviews.

PT: I'm not sure. I slept in their room until I was five. I was in
    a crib for a long time. I can't remember. I can't remember. I

never thought about that before. I don't remember. (At this point the patient became very agitated.)

DR: What else comes to your mind?

PT: When I was young, my father used to take me to bed and tell me stories. I didn't even think about that. I was very little. He used to sing songs to me. If we got cut, he used to take mercurochrome and draw pictures on my arm if I got cut. I remember once my father being very mad and yelling at me real loud. He just yelled so loud at me when I was in the crib.

The next morning in an interview with the medical student, the patient revealed another new bit of information. At the end of the week during which her father had been making friendly overtures to her, and the night before the outbreak of her anxiety attacks with the associated frightening images of sexual activity with her father, she had had a nightmare. On the surface the content of the dream seemed harmless enough: She was, she dreamed, at a zoo. It was nighttime, and she heard funny noises in the darkness. She asked a zoo attendant standing next to her what the noises were. He replied, "Oh, that's only the animals mating." She then noticed in front of her a large grey elephant lying on its right side on the grass. It was moving its left hind leg up and down as if it were trying to get up. At that point she awoke in terror and experienced the outbreak of her symptoms.

In the third and final therapeutic interview, the patient was seen by the student and supervisor together. The latter focused the patient's attention on the elements of the dream and systematically elicited her associations to them. The result was the recovery of a long-forgotten, repressed childhood memory dating back to the fourth or fifth year of her life: While sleeping in the crib in her parents' bedroom, she awoke one night and saw them naked, engaged in sexual intercourse. Suddenly they noticed her watching and sprang apart. The patient remembered seeing her mother hastily pull the bedclothes up around her, and her father roll over, half on his back, half on his left side. She noticed his erection, and then saw him lift up his left leg, sit up, and yell at her crossly to go to sleep. At this point she ducked down, hid her head under the covers, and pretended to doze off.

It was not easy for the patient to describe this scene as the memories emerged. She stammered, hesitated, and spoke in a low, tremulous voice with intense shame and anxiety. After discharging a large quantity of affect, she gradually became more composed and was able to return to the ward. Afterward, her symptoms totally vanished, she became more cheerful and outgoing on the ward, and it was possible to discharge her a few days therafter. Two months later, when seen in a followup visit in the outpatient clinic, she reported that she was asymptomatic and feeling fine.

To recapitulate, we are presented with a young woman whose primary complaint was severe, disabling attacks of anxiety associated with overtly incestuous fantasies. On psychodynamic exploration, however, it became evident that the anxiety itself was the surface manifestation of a complex psychic structure of partly conscious and partly unconscious mental elements—the memory of a traumatic event, unresolved incestuous feelings for her father leading to wish-fulfilling fantasies of sexual activity, and psychological defenses erected against these forbidden drives, affects, and thoughts. The anxiety represented the internal reaction of her ego (and superego) to the pressure from the underlying drive, and acted as the motivation for erecting the defenses of repression, avoidance, and reaction-formation aimed at pushing and keeping the drives out of conscious awareness so that she might avoid experiencing the painful anxiety. A psychological equilibrium among the conflicting mental forces was thereby established.

For a number of years this equilibrium remained stable, and the patient was able to marry and to lead a life of her own unhampered by neurotic symptoms or problems. In the course of events, however, the balance of equilibrium was upset by the environmental stress imposed by the father's attempts to move closer to the patient in a kind of loving offer to help her financially. As a result, the underlying incestuous drive was stimulated and thus aroused, threatened to escape the control of the defenses that had until then successfully contained it. The emergence of the drive into consciousness was only partial, however, and was manifested by the appearance of an *ego-alien* symptom in the form of disturbing sexual imagery that obtruded itself into the patient's thoughts. The patient still did not recognize the drive as her own wish, was made acutely anxious by the imagery, and intensified her defensive maneuvers to contain and repress it. Nevertheless, the defenses were only partially successful, and though the full force and range of the drive (and the early memories associated with it) still remained unconscious, the patient's psychic equilibrium was now altered and her psychic structure and function was pathologically distorted. As a result, neurotic symptoms developed that seriously compromised the patient's relationships and capacity to carry on with the normal activities of her daily life.

Freud's Views and Modern Theory

In this psychodynamic model of neurotic symptom formation, anxiety is viewed as playing a central role both as an ego affect in response to the threatened emergence into consciousness of frightening repressed mental elements, and as a motivating force for the erection of ego defenses to contain the forbidden drives, affects, and fantasies. This, of course, is the classical psychoanalytic conception of the nature and function of anxiety (2). It should be remembered, however, that in his earliest clinical psychoanalytic writings, Freud advanced a view of anxiety that was quite different and that has often been lost sight of in the more traditional concept of the signal function of anxiety (3,4).

Although not identical to the model of symptom formation just presented, Freud's early explanation of hysteria involved the notion of psychic structure and psychic conflict. The hysterical symptom, he proposed, resulted from the repression of the libidinal drive with its associated cognitive and affective components and its *conversion* into a sensorimotor symptom that symbolically represented and expressed the underlying repressed unconscious elements (5,6).

When he turned his attention to the problem of anxiety, Freud proposed a formulation that did not invoke the psychic elaboration and structure he found in the production of the hysterical symptom (3). Although as in hysteria, the sexual drive was involved in the appearance of anxiety, the mechanism of symptom formation was different. Anxiety resulted when the sexual drive could not be discharged in normal sexual activity, whether as a result of continence, coitus interruptus, or other factors that blocked full sexual discharge. The libidinal energy, blocked from such discharge, was directly transformed into anxiety without undergoing any form of psychic elaboration. "The anxiety neurosis," Freud writes, "has a sexual origin ... but it does not attach itself to ideas taken from sexual life; properly speaking, it has no psychical mechanism. Its specific cause is the accumulation of sexual tension, produced by abstinence or by unconsummated sexual excitation" (4).

"The clinical symptoms of anxiety can be traced to no psychical origin....The mechanism of anxiety neurosis is to be looked for in a deflection of sexual excitation from the psychical sphere and in a consequent abnormal employment of that excitation....Anxiety neurosis is created by everything which keeps somatic sexual tension away from the psychic sphere, which interferes with its being worked over psychically....The affect does not originate in a repressed idea, but turns out to be not further reducible by psychological analysis, nor amenable to psychotherapy"(3).

To summarize, Freud proposes here that anxiety is not the result of psychological processes, that it does not involve any higher order psychic structure or mechanisms, but that it represents the direct biological transformation of sexual arousal into the somatic manifestations of autonomic discharge. Freud, furthermore, made a close association between agoraphobia and anxiety neurosis. "In the case of agoraphobia," he writes, "we often find the recollection of an anxiety attack, and what the patient actually fears is the occurrence of such an attack under the special conditions in which he believes he cannot escape it"(4).

Later in the development of analytic theory, with the introduction of the structural model of psychic functioning, anxiety is conceived as a basically psychological phenomenon (2). As *signal* anxiety, it is seen as central to psychic conflict and to the erection of psychological defenses. As noted earlier, the more biological concept of anxiety was almost completely lost sight of in later psychoanalytic theoretical formulations. It is interesting, therefore, to find Freud's early ideas about anxiety now being revived and supported by modern clinical observations and psychopharmacological investigations (7-9). These have produced a number of new findings and concepts of scientific and therapeutic merit such as, for example, the pharmacological dissection of panic anxiety from anticipatory anxiety, the seeming absence of psychological mechanisms in the production of many panic attacks, the relation of such attacks to the subsequent emergence of the secondary anticipatory anxiety that is central to the development of agoraphobia, and the therapeutic usefulness of medications in controlling panic. Freud's concept of the dual nature of anxiety is remarkably similar to modern formulations.

Another line of modern clinical investigation has similar points of contact with Freud's early views about anxiety. Over the past decade, psychological observation of patients with classical psychosomatic disorders has defined a psychological syndrome, termed "alexithymia," (10,11) which appears to be significantly correlated with the psychosomatic process. Two central features characterize the alexithymic syndrome: (a) an inability of such patients to describe their feelings or to differentiate among them; and (b) an absence of the capacity to produce fantasies with the result that the thought content of such patients is restricted to a preoccupation with *external* objects, people, and environmental events. Their thought content, in other words, tends to be stimulus bound rather than drive determined.

To understand and appreciate the full range of alexithymic behavior, one must observe the details of a clinical interview with an alexithymic individual. The short excerpts from a video-recorded interview that follow give some idea of its central features. The patient, a married man in his mid-twenties, was in the hospital for the recurrence of symptoms referable to a peptic ulcer that had previously resulted in a duodenal perforation requiring emergency surgery. The initial phase of the interview was focused on the history of the patient's illness and the environmental stresses that were correlated with its onset and exacerbation. The patient spoke fluently and at length about these external events, providing the interviewer with a clear picture of the course of his illness and the surgical treatment, as well as of the stresses imposed on him by overwork, financial problems, and his wife's chronic, debilitating illness and hospitalization. However, when the doctor inquired about the patient's emotional response to his problems, especially his wife's current illness, there was a striking change in the pace of the interview:

DR: (referring to the patient's wife's recent two-month hospitalization) How did you feel about that?
PT: About her being in the hospital? Well, I did have quite a few problems with, you know, relating myself to the problems she had. I had something of a tendency to blame myself for it.
DR: How? In what way? How did you blame yourself?
PT: (Long pause.) It would be hard to say. I just—uh—(pause) I really couldn't say. (silence)

The patient's inarticulateness and remarkable inability to describe his inner feelings is further illustrated in a later portion of the interview, which demonstrates, too, his lack of fantasies and inability to differentiate among affects. The patient had been *describing* in some detail his wife's dependent, demanding behavior when she was sick (external events). This, he said, made him feel "bad."

DR: Could you describe that feeling for me?
PT: (long pause) Mostly just a guilty feeling.
DR: Guilty?
PT: Yes.
DR: And how did you experience that? How did you feel that?
PT: Well, I really couldn't tell you how it would manifest itself.
DR: Were there other feelings that went along with it? Or with the trouble that you were in?
PT: Not really. (silence)

Once more, in this portion of the interview we find the same sequence of events. The patient is able to talk fluently enough about external happenings and persons, and volunteers the fact that he felt "bad" about the situation. However, when asked to describe the bad feeling, he becomes inarticulate and the interview again comes to a halt. The doctor then focused the interview on the behavior of the patient's wife. In response, the patient described readily his wife's demanding, dependent behavior when she was sick, and the interview continued as follows:

DR: How would you feel then?

PT: Well, I'd get mad.

DR: What was it like when you got mad? What did that feel like?

PT: Well, pretty much just a pent up anger. I really wouldn't express it too much, you know. It is mostly pretty much a pent up feeling inside myself.

DR: What did it feel like? Can you describe it? What is the pent up feeling?

PT: Well, I guess just generally I wouldn't be able to relax physically, you know. Most of the time I would be tight, and I might feel something of an upset stomach.

DR: And, what would that feel like—the upset stomach?

PT: Well, something close to nausea, I guess.

DR: What kind of thoughts would you have when you'd be angry or be mad?

PT: Well, I'd go into something of a depression sometimes.

DR: What do you mean by that? I am just trying to understand what you experience.

PT: Well, I might get angry about something, you know, and have a completely unfulfilled feeling about it. I couldn't express my anger in any way, and it would just stay inside for quite a long time afterward. I couldn't express it, you know, in just letting it out. And I also couldn't just, you know, get it to go away.

DR: And that would lead to a sad feeling, you say? How did that differ from feeling angry—feeling sad?

PT: Well, I'd just have a hard time enjoying myself doing anything. I like to read a lot. I wouldn't be able to get into what I'd be reading. Just have some trouble, you know, applying myself to anything.

DR: And when you'd feel sad, would you feel that anywhere in your body?

PT: Well, still also something of an upset stomach thing.

DR: So how could you tell the difference between that and being angry? Being sad and being angry?

PT: (long pause) Well, anger at first would be much more of a stronger feeling, I guess. I don't know how many different ways you can be angry. This is just a pretty standard thing, isn't it?

DR: No, but I mean the difference between being angry and being sad. You said you'd be angry and then you'd be sad. I was trying to understand how you could tell the difference between being angry and being sad.

PT: Well, anger would be just a stronger thing. It is just a feeling of anger. I don't know how much more I could say.

DR: When you feel angry, what kind of thoughts would go along with it?

PT: Well—(pause) It was just whatever the situation would be. That is what would be on my mind, of course.

DR: For example?

PT: Well, sometimes, for instance, like I mentioned before, having a problem with my wife demanding a lot of attention. What feelings would go along with it?

DR: What thoughts would you have when you'd get angry at that situation, mad at that situation?

PT: Well, I'd just be, I'd just be mad at both her and myself. I don't know.

Two observations are noteworthy in this segment of the interview. First, the interviewer is unable to elicit any fantasies of angry behavior despite directly questioning the patient about his thoughts in connection with being "mad." Instead, the patient responds by referring to another feeling ("depression"). A moment later he reports that his thoughts are about the situation that made him "mad"—that is, about external events, not fantasied angry actions. Second, we find the same difficulty in describing feelings that we have observed before, but with an interesting addition: The patient appears to experience both anger and sadness (depression) in an identical sensation referred to his stomach—a feeling of nausea. When specifically requested to differentiate these two feelings, he is unable to do so. The same phenomenon was evident a bit later in the interview when the patient was asked for clarification of what he referred to as "tension."

DR: Could you describe the tension?

PT: Well—(long silence)

DR: Do you feel it anywhere in your body?

PT: It is also a stomach feeling too....Pretty much the same feeling I had with anger.

Let us summarize the nature of these observations. It is evident that the patient is responding to environmental stress with an unpleasant but ill-defined state of internal arousal. However, despite the fact that he uses different verbal labels ("mad," "tension," "depression"), experientially these terms do not define differentiated feeling states but all refer to the same uncomfortable sensation in his stomach. Without fantasies to indicate the quality of his affects (e.g., gloomy, fearful, or angry thoughts) and without differences in the description of how they are experienced, the observer as well as the patient is unable to determine how they differ from one another.

Although not apparent from a verbal transcript of a videotaped interview, the patient gave no visible evidence of emotion throughout the entire interchange. His posture was wooden, his facial expression was bland and unchanging, and his tone of voice was flat and unmodulated. The only change of pace in the interview occurred during the periods of slowing of his associations (often to the point of complete silence) when he was questioned about the nature of his feelings, or when the interviewer tried to elicit fantasies. Furthermore, the interviewer often felt a sense of boredom in the face of the remarkable poverty, aridity, shallowness, and drab banality of the patient's productions and responses.

If we compare the behavior of this patient (and others with similar alexithymic characteristics) with neurotic patients like the young woman whose struggle with incestuous thoughts was described earlier, we find interesting points of difference. The neurotic patient exhibits a rich inner life of varied and differentiated feelings, of fantasies, of memories, of imagery, all of which are woven by associative links into a complex psychic structure that is partly conscious, partly unconscious. The full extent of the structure can be uncovered through careful psychological exploration that brings previously unconscious material into conscious awareness. This awareness discloses a conflict among the various elements of the structure that results in an equilibrium among the conflicting forces whose surface manifestation is seen in the compromise-formation of neurotic symptoms, behavior, and relationships.

In the alexithymic individual, on the other hand, the rich, variegated, complex psychic structure that characterizes the neurotic patient is not to be found. Psychological examination reveals a mental content that is unimaginative, lacking in fantasies, pragmatic, and preoccupied with the numerous small, mundane details of external events and things. The individual's emotional life is shallow; he has no vocabulary with which to describe feelings, often appears not to experience emotions at all, nor to understand what the words feeling and emotion mean. If he is aware of inner emotional discomfort, he is unable to distinguish differentiated, qualitatively distinct emotional states.

Psychosomatic Symptom Formation

Conflict Model

Early psychosomatic investigators, especially Alexander and his colleagues (12), recognized the lack of cognitive elements in the formation of psychosomatic symptoms (as opposed to neurotic, hysterical symptom formation) and ascribed their development to the repression of affect alone. In this theoretical formulation (which retained the traditional concept of psychological structure and conflict that had been derived from the observation of neurotic patients), repression was seen as removing affect from conscious awareness and discharge, with a resulting chronic arousal of the autonomic nervous system leading eventually to lesions in the autonomic end-organs stimulated by the chronic autonomic discharge.

The conflict model provided a reasonable and possible hypothesis to explain psychosomatic symptom formation. Its universal applicability, however, was brought into question by subsequent clinical experience. As psychoanalytic therapeutic techniques were increasingly applied to patients with psychosomatic disorders, it became evident that many if not most of them were unable to follow the required procedures (13,14). They could not associate like neurotic patients, they were unable to talk about feelings or fantasies, and they maintained a stubborn, unchanging inability to recognize internal psychological conflicts or problems despite the attempts of skilled therapists to uncover emotional factors. Such patients were often puzzled by the psychotherapeutic procedures required of them, would drop out of treatment prematurely, or if they completed a course of therapy, emerged without any change of internal psychic structure or without any greater degree of awareness of psychological processes than that with which they began psychotherapy.

Deficit Model

Given the failure of psychological exploration to reveal in such patients the presence of unconscious feelings and fantasies predicted by the conflict hypothesis (a hypothesis long amply substantiated for neurotic symptoms by the uncovering of unconscious factors in symptom formation), clinical investigators of the psychosomatic process more recently suggested that the conflict model does not necessarily apply for all instances of psychosomatic symptom formation (15). Instead, they suggest that the symptoms are often the manifestations of ego *deficits* in the capacity for fantasy production and for experiencing and differentiating affects—whether these deficits are the result of disturbances in early growth and development (16) or of regression (17) from more mature forms of psychological functioning.

The substitution of a *deficit* model for a *conflict* model of symptom formation is important for understanding and explaining the production of stress-related illness. It suggests that psychic arousal produced by stressful environmental events may be processed by at least two different internal mechanisms. In this expanded explanatory scheme, neurotic symptoms are viewed as the result of the modification of stress-induced arousal over a complex structure of conscious and unconscious psychological processes. If, however, such a psychic structure is not available to transform the stress-induced arousal into neurotic symptoms, it is discharged directly over autonomic channels, resulting in somatic symptoms that are correlated with no higher order psychic processes or representations.

The deficit model of psychosomatic symptom formation is remarkably similar to Freud's earliest concept of the production of anxiety; that is, that it results from a direct translation of internal arousal into somatic pathways of discharge without any modification by higher order psychic processes. In this theoretical framework, one may view panic anxiety as a psychosomatic disorder—perhaps, even, as the prototypical psychosomatic disorder representing the transformation of stress-induced arousal into a *generalized* autonomic discharge. If the discharge of the stress-related arousal is canalized and restricted to more discrete autonomic pathways, specific, localized peripheral psychosomatic symptoms in the target end-organ will result. In other words, psychosomatic symptoms—whether in the form of generalized panic anxiety or localized diseases of specific organs (peptic ulcer, e.g.)—occur when the pathways of higher psychic structure underlying neurotic symptom formation are unavailable for the discharge of stress-induced internal arousal. Without that higher structure, stress is directly transformed into somatic symptoms through a short-circuiting of arousal into autonomic channels.

Therapeutic Approaches

With these theoretical formulations in mind, let us turn to a brief consideration of the therapeutic approach to anxiety. The development of behavioral desensitization techniques and the more recent discovery of the effectiveness of antidepressant medications in controlling panic attacks have greatly strengthened the psychiatrist's ability to help patients with disabling anxiety symptoms. At the same time, these therapeutic advances, especially in the biological sphere, have put our knowledge of the psychological determinants of anxiety in the shade. A tendency exists among many modern clinicians to think of anxiety as a purely biological disorder and to treat it accordingly. This narrowness of vision leads to an unfortunate disregard of the evidence suggesting that anxiety may be the result of more than one underlying mechanism, and that the therapeutic approach or approaches should be based on a careful clinical assessment of the etiology of the symptoms.

Pharmacotherapy vs. Psychotherapy

Recent investigation provides knowledge that some patients may have a biological diathesis for the development of debilitating panic attacks that requires a pharmacological stabilization of the underlying neurochemical imbalance to bring the symptoms under control. The clinical findings that in some patients panic attacks occur without any evidence of environmental stress or other psychological dysfunction lends credence to the claim that anxiety symptoms may be endogenous and are primarily the result of purely biological processes. Clearly, pharmacotherapy is the treatment of choice in such cases.

Conversely, clinical experience teaches us that for some patients who present with isolated panic attacks that are seemingly unrelated to environmental or psychological factors, skilled psychodynamic explorations eventually will reveal initially repressed, unconscious conflicts that are important in the genesis of the anxiety. In such patients, a combination of insight psychotherapy *and* medication to control disabling panic may provide a treatment more lastingly effective than using either therapeutic approach alone. For an alexithymic individual without the capacity for higher psychic elaboration, endogenous panic attacks may represent a response to environmental stress involving the direct psychosomatic transformation of the resulting internal arousal into autonomic discharge. The absence of psychic conflict in such patients can be determined only by clinical observation based on psychoanalytic knowledge. This in turn provides the grounds for judging that psychoanalytically oriented insight psychotherapy is contraindicated, and that appropriate therapy should combine medication with supportive measures and environmental manipulation designed either to reduce the environmental stress or to remove the patient from it.

Psychodynamic and Biological Synthesis

The indications for the various therapeutic approaches suggested here must be viewed as tentative at best, since our knowledge of the factors that produce anxiety is far from complete. Perhaps the only thing that may be said with certainty is that the ultimate conception and treatment of anxiety must be based on a synthesis of both biological and psychodynamic factors. Without psychodynamic observation, we cannot determine the nature of the various pathways by which stress is transformed into symptoms. Without knowledge of the underlying biological mechanisms, we cannot elucidate the structural basis for the activation and functioning of those pathways. And without a combination of both, we shall remain unable to provide our patients with rational, comprehensive, and effective treatment.

References

1. Breuer J, Freud S: Studies on hysteria in Complete Psychological Works, standard ed, vol 2. Translated and edited by Strachey J. London, Hogarth Press, pp 3-305, 1955

2. Freud S: Inhibitions, symptoms and anxiety, in Complete Psychological Works, standard ed, vol 20. Translated and edited by Strachey J. London, Hogarth Press, 1959, pp 87-172

3. Freud S: On the grounds for detaching a particular syndrome from neurasthenia under the description "anxiety neurosis," in Complete Psychological Works, standard ed, vol 3. Translated and edited by Strachey J. London, Hogarth Press, 1962, pp 90-115

4. Freud S: Obsessions and phobias, in Complete Psychological Works, standard ed, vol 3. Translated and edited by Strachey J. London, Hogarth Press, 1962, pp 74-82

5. Breuer J, Freud S: On the psychical mechanism of hysterical phenomena: preliminary communication, in Complete Psychological Works, standard ed, vol 2. Translated and edited by Strachey J. London, Hogarth Press, 1955, pp 3-17

6. Freud S: The neuro-psychoses of defence, in Complete Psychological Works, standard ed, vol 3. London, Hogarth Press, 1962, pp 45-61

7. Group for the Advancement of Psychiatry (GAP): Committee on Research, Pharmacotherapy and Psychotherapy: Paradoxes, Problems and Progress, vol IX, report #93. New York Mental Health Materials Center, 1975, pp 259-434

8. Klein D, Rabkin J: Anxiety: New Research and Changing Concepts. New York, Raven Press, 1981

9. Sheehan D: Panic attacks and phobias. New Engl J Med 307:156-158, 1982

10. Sifneos P: The prevalence of "alexithymic" characteristics in psychosomatic patients. Psychother Psychosom 22:255-262, 1973

11. Nemiah J: Alexithymia and psychosomatic illness. JCE Psychiatry, October 1978, pp 25-37

12. Alexander F: Fundamental concepts of psychosomatic research. Psychosom Med 5:205-210, 1943

13. Karush A, Daniels G: The response of psychotherapy in chronic ulcerative colitis. Psychosom Med 31:201-227, 1969

14. Nemiah J: The psychological management and treatment of patients with peptic ulcer. Adv Psychosom Med 6:169-185, 1971

15. Nemiah J: Alexithymia: theoretical considerations. Psychother Psychosom 28:199-206, 1977

16. McDougall J: The psychosoma and the psychoanalytic process. Int Rev Psychoanal 1:437, 1974

17. Krystal H, Raskin H: Drug dependence: aspects of ego functions. Detroit, Wayne State University Press, 1970

6

Strategies for Diagnosis and Treatment of Anxiety Disorder

David Sheehan, M.D.

6

Strategies for Diagnosis and Treatment of Anxiety Disorders

David Sheehan, M.D.

Introduction

Anxiety disorders are a heterogeneous group of problems. To treat them effectively it is first necessary to have a diagnostic system that clearly distinguishes each of these groups from one another. A good diagnostic system should also direct the clinician to the treatment that is most likely to be effective for each patient.

The severe anxiety disorder associated with panic attacks and phobic symptoms lends itself to diagnostic confusion. It is a multidimensional disorder that can manifest itself in many different parts of the body. Focusing on one of its symptoms to the exclusion of the overall cluster can be very misleading, because these isolated symptoms can mimic so many other illnesses. This can lead to repeated consultations and costly workups. In the past the disorder has been given a large number of different diagnostic labels, usually reflecting the specialty or theoretical orientation of the diagnostician. Well-known examples include cardiac neurosis, panic disorder, agoraphobia, anxiety neurosis, and depersonalization disorder, and hyperventilation syndrome.

As mentioned in Chapter 1, the third edition of the *Diagnostic and Statistical Manual of Mental Disorders* (DSM-III) (1) has helped clarify most of the past diagnostic confusion in psychiatry by (a) its recommendation of a multiaxial diagnostic system and (b) setting down precisely defined criteria for each diagnostic category. In the multiaxial diagnostic system, each patient receives a diagnosis along each of five axes as follows:

Axis 1 - A diagnosis of the clinical psychiatric
    syndrome based on the clinical
    description of symptoms and signs.
Axis 2 - A personality disorder diagnosis based on
    the individual's character structure and
    mode of interaction with his environment.
Axis 3 - Diagnosis of medical (nonpsychiatric)
    problems.
Axis 4 - Severity of psychosocial stressors.
Axis 5 - Highest level of adaptive functioning
    in prior year (the goal of treatment
    presumably being to restore the patient
    to at least this level).

The focus of this chapter will be based on Axis 1, diagnostic classification of anxiety disorders based on a description and clustering of the symptoms and signs.

Goals of Classification

The immediate goal of a classification system is to organize systematically the phenomena into groups in which members of each group have common characteristics. The reason for this is to achieve an economy of memory. As applied to medical science, the symptoms, signs, demography, pathophysiology, etiology, natural history, family history, and treatment response would be similar within each group and would differ from one group to the next.

The long-term purpose of a good classification system is to enhance prediction. In the case of medical science, the diagnostic class the patient falls into should help to predict other symptoms, complications that may develop in the future, and above all the best treatment for the patient. Better prediction should enhance our ability to anticipate, manipulate, and control the disorder. A classification system should also clarify phenomena that would otherwise appear disconnected and diverse.

The Elements of a Good Classification System

A good classification system should accommodate the following key elements:

1. The classes inherently should be mutually exclusive, i.e., there should be little significant overlap between the classes and each class should be as distinct as possible from the next.
2. The classes should be internally homogeneous, i.e., internal consistency and homogeneity should exist within each class (diagnostic category).
3. The classification system should be comprehensive, i.e., it should have a category to accommodate all cases encountered.
4. It should permit better prediction and control.
5. It should clarify rather than confuse.
6. It should be simple, clear, and precise and should offer an economy of memory.
7. The number of groups should be manageable.
8. The characteristics in each group should be preponderantly constant.
9. Each group should possess the property of "naturalness" to the highest possible degree. A "natural" group is one in which all elements share the large majority (x) of a large number of features (y). The elements of each group "may have any combination of features as long as the total number of features shared with every other element of the set is x or more"(2).

For example, DSM-III (in anxiety-related diagnoses) selects only a few elements of a group to the exclusion of the many other symptoms and elevates these to the level of a "natural" class. It is as if in the process, it "carves nature at the joints." The many anxiety (and other) symptoms around panic attacks constitute panic disorder, yet agoraphobia, with all of the same symptoms, is made a different class. Similarly, social phobia, hypochondriasis, depersonalization disorder, and generalized anxiety disorder—all of which share a majority of symptoms with panic disorder most of the time—are each in turn elevated to a class of their own, as if each in turn were an independent, naturally occurring class in its own right. In reality it is just as likely that they are each only an "unnatural" part of the single class of biological anxiety disease.

The gaps between the mutually exclusive classes must not contain a chain of intermediate elements that are more numerous than the extreme forms of the mutually exclusive classes. Hierarchical natural groups should be made on only the basis of known and already identified clusters of elements. This is most clear when dealing with elements that fall into two distinct clusters. The two clusters would be two classes in a classification scheme. However, if it is later found that these two classes are connected by a chain of intermediate elements which are more numerous than the extreme forms, this would constitute a single cluster. We would now have to consider this cluster as a single class (2). This has special bearing on the many diagnostic categories relating to anxiety in DSM-III. Many of these anxiety-related diagnoses appear to be extreme forms. In clinical practice they seem to be connected by a large number of intermediate types of patients with a mixture of elements, parts of which are shared in common with several of the extreme groups. For this reason it may be better to collapse these many extreme groups into one or two clusters.

Some of these criteria for a good classification system deserve more weight than others. Special importance should be given to having classes that inherently are mutually exclusive and to disallowing significant category overlap. If a classification system for anxiety disorders fails on this criterion, further consideration of that classification on other criteria is redundant.

Approaches to Classification

Taxonomy, the study of classification according to natural relationships, is a growing branch of science with a wide array of principles and techniques to call on. The many approaches to setting up a classification system for anxiety disorders might be broadly grouped into the "theological" approach and the "scientific" approach. The theological approach is to distill the collective wisdom of a group of experts and accept their views as authoritative, whereas the scientific approach uses a number of statistical methods on data from anxious patients.

One scientific approach would involve two exploratory stages and a final testing or confirmatory stage. The first exploratory stage calls for a cluster analysis of symptoms in a population of anxious patients. The cluster analysis attempts to separate the symptoms into distinct groups. The second stage calls for a discriminant analysis on these clusters to determine the symptoms with the highest discriminating power between the identified clusters. These discriminators then become the diagnostic criteria for each class in the classification system. The final confirmatory stage requires that these discriminating variables be tested on a fresh patient population to see how well they comprehensively assign all cases into mutually exclusive groups. No matter what approach is used to develop a classification system, it is necessary to put it to the test with this final confirmatory stage. The classification must be forced to face reality to see how well it fits.

Problems with Existing Classifications
of Anxiety Disorders

Table 6-1 provides an extensive list of diagnostic labels collected from the medical records of 57 patients in a study for the treatment of panic attacks and multiple phobias (3). Despite the diversity of diagnostic labels they had attracted over the prior 20 years, all the diagnoses had been assigned to the same set of symptoms. This list includes several diagnoses from DSM-II (1950) as well as others that found

Table 6-1. Diagnostic Labels Synonymous with Endogenous Anxiety

---

ANXIETY HYSTERIA

Hysteria (early descriptions)
Globus hystericus
Grand hysterie
Hysterical neurosis
Vertigo hysterique

ANXIETY NEUROSIS

Anxiety syndrome
Pseudoneurosis
Borderline states
Locomotor anxiety
Anxiety states
Severe mixed neurosis
Pseudoneurotic schizophrenia
Nonspecific insecurity fears
Street fear

PHOBIC ANXIETY STATE

PHOBIC ANXIETY DEPERSONALIZATION SYNDROME

Separation anxiety
Effort syndrome
Phobophobia
Severe school phobia
Irritable heart syndrome

DA COSTA'S SYNDROME

Cardiac neurosis
Hyperdynamic beta-adrenergic circulatory state
Nervous tachycardia
Neurocirculatory asthenia
Soldier's heart
Autonomic epilepsy
Vasomotor neurosis
Vasoregulatory asthenia

HYPERVENTILATION SYNDROME

Panic disorders
Autonomic epilepsy
"Hypoglycemic" syndrome
Hypochondriacal neurosis
Depersonalization neurosis

ATYPICAL DEPRESSION

Depressive anxiety states

Source: Sheehan, DV, et al., 1980. Reprinted with permission.

historical favor with various groups. However, until the establishment of criteria by Feighner and others (4), Spitzer and others (5), and DSM-III, there were no precisely defined criteria for any of these diagnostic labels that could be used to permit comparison of diagnoses from one center to another. Although overall DSM-III represents a positive step toward diagnostic precision, it allows that precision to be misplaced while sorting out the diagnostic confusion in anxiety and phobic disorders. This has been reviewed at length elsewhere (6,7).

The problems with DSM-III diagnoses relating to anxiety may be summed up as follows:

1. There are 21 to 25 diagnostic categories in DSM-III to which an anxious patient might reasonably be assigned (6,7) (Table 6-2). Depending on the theoretical orienta-

Table 6-2. Possible Coexistence of DSM-III Anxiety-Related Diagnoses

```
 1 PANIC DISORDER                          I
 2 GENERALIZED ANXIETY DISORDER           -2
 3 ATYPICAL ANXIETY DISORDER              • - -3
 4 ADJUSTMENT DIS. C ANXIOUS MOOD          - - -4
 5 AGORAPHOBIA C PANIC ATTACKS             - - - -5
 6 AGORAPHOBIA O PANIC ATTACKS             - + - - -6
 7 SOCIAL PHOBIA                           + + - - + +7
 8 SIMPLE PHOBIA                           + + - - + + +8
 9 AVOIDANCE PERSONALITY DISORDER          + + + - + + + +9
10 SOMATIZATION DISORDER                   + - + - + + + + +10
11 CONVERSION DISORDER                     + + + - + + + + + -11
12 ATYPICAL SOMATOFORM DISORDER            + + + - + + + + + - -12
13 DEPERSONALIZATION DISORDER              - - - - - - - - + + + +13
14 HYPOCHONDRIASIS                         - - + - + + + + + - + - +14
15 HISTRIONIC PERSONALITY DISORDER         + + + - + + + + + + + + + +15
16 POSTTRAUMATIC STRESS DISORDER           + + - + + + + + + + + + - -+ 16
17 OBSESSIVE COMPULSIVE DISORDER           - - - - - - + - + + + + - -+ +17
18 ATYPICAL DISSOCIATIVE DISORDER          + + + - - + + + + + + + - + + + +18
19 SEPARATING ANXIETY DISORDER             + + - - + + + + + + + + - + + + ++19
20 AVOIDANCE DIS. OF CHILDHOOD/ADOL.       + + + - + + + + - + + + - + + + + + +20
21 OVERANXIOUS DISORDER                    + + - - - - - - - + + + - + + + -+ - -21
```

Key: − = Combination not allowed
+ = Combination allowed
138 Combinations permitted

tion or specialty interest of the physician, any one or more of the patient's symptoms might be selected and a diagnosis assigned around that cluster.

2. To add flexibility (and further confusion) to this range of choices, DSM-III recognizes that some of these diagnostic categories may coexist. Careful examination of DSM-III finds that there are 138 possible combinations of such diagnoses allowed (1,6,7). The number of groups, whether it is 21 or 138, is clearly unmanageable.

3. There is significant category overlap among these groups, and they cannot be realistically considered as inherently mutually exclusive (6,7). In the absence of inherently mutually exclusive categories, further empirical investigation is complicated. Statistically valid analysis of nominal data and especially any useful multivariate analysis will be difficult to justify because the basic assumption of many statistical tests is that the variables under study are independent from each other.

4. The DSM-III anxiety-related classification is neither simple nor clear, and it fails to provide an economy of memory.

5. The symptom characteristics of each DSM-III anxiety group are not preponderantly constant. For example, the generalized anxiety disorder of today may become the panic disorder of next month, the social phobia of next year, and the agoraphobia of several years hence.

6. Many of the DSM-III groups do not possess the property of naturalness described earlier. Depersonalization disorder, for example, may only be an unnatural part of the single class of biological anxiety disease.

7. It seems likely that the gaps between the DSM-III anxiety diagnostic clusters contain a chain of intermediate elements that are more numerous than the extreme forms of the existing diagnostic groups.

8. The decision tree aids to differential diagnosis of anxiety and phobias (appendix A in DSM-III) are an attempt to clarify and simplify some of the problems that arise from the text alone. They do not, however, allow for the possible coexistence of diagnoses as does the text. For example, the DSM-III text states that "agoraphobia or

simple phobia may coexist with social phobia" (1). The decision tree does not allow for this. It does not accommodate the idea that severe endogenous anxiety disorder fluctuates, remits, recurs, and may manifest itself in a variety of apparently different ways at different times during the chronic course of the disorder. If DSM-III is strictly followed, the diagnosis will change frequently in these patients over the course of time. Allowing such frequent diagnostic changes in the same patient for essentially the same condition permits unnecessary confusion. On the other hand, should the first significant category the patient is assigned to during the course of his or her illness be the one we settle on thereafter?

On the positive side, DSM-III does appear to be comprehensive, that is, it provides a category to accommodate all cases encountered. It also appears to provide categories that are internally homogenous.

The Impact of Classification on Clinical Practice: A Case Illustration

A 21-year-old woman presents with a two-year history that began with episodes where everything around her became strange, unreal, detached, and unfamiliar, sufficient to satisfy DSM-III criteria for a diagnosis of depersonalization disorder. One year later she became hypochondriacal about fleeting symptoms in her chest (e.g., left-sided chest pressure even when she did not feel anxious) and consulted many physicians to rule out heart disease. Her preoccupation and fear that she had heart disease persisted in spite of many reassurances. Seen at this stage she would have satisfied diagnostic criteria in DSM-III for hypochondriasis.

Six months later the patient had increased tension, anxiety, and automatic hyperactivity sufficient to be called generalized anxiety disorder (DSM-III). Two months later she choked on food while feeling anxious and subsequently avoided eating solid foods. This would earn the diagnosis of simple phobia (DSM-III) since at this juncture that was her main concern. During the following two months this fear generalized. She feared eating with friends, going to restaurants, being watched by her family while eating, and being the focus of attention. Consequently, she began eating alone in her bedroom. The patient had a social phobia. A week later she was seen by a psychiatrist who diagnosed her condition as a conversion disorder. Her main complaint to him was a persistent lump in the throat that prevented her from swallowing normally. In the past that would have been called globus hystericus.

One week later the patient had an intense dizzy spell while driving on a highway some distance from her home. For the next week she was too frightened to leave her house. This would have justified a DSM-III diagnosis of agoraphobia without panic attacks. Shortly, she started going out again and regaining her confidence, overcoming these phobias. Some weeks later, however, she had a series of typical spontaneous panic attacks (panic disorder in DSM-III), and within a week she was again housebound by her fears. At this point the patient has all of the features of agoraphobia with panic attacks (DSM-III).

When she was diagnosed as having a generalized anxiety disorder, would a benzodiazepine be recommended? Wouldn't behavior therapy and exposure in vivo have been the logical treatments when she earned the diagnosis of simple or social phobia? With a diagnosis of conversion disorder, wouldn't conventional practice call for psychotherapy or hypnosis? Weeks later, with her eighth diagnosis—panic disorder—in two years, wouldn't imipramine be a logical solution to her problem?

When we examine this case cross sectionally at different stages during the past two years, we take a different view of her clinical syndrome and its etiology, and are guided to a different choice of treatment. Such a cross-sectional view of the case may be quite misleading. It does not make much sense to presume that this patient has had nine different diseases in two years. A more precise classification is to consider the case longitudinally as one disease passing through several stages.

Natural History: The March of Panic

Typical patients with endogenous anxiety usually describe several stages in the natural progression of their illness over a number of years.

Stage 1 - Subpanic symptom attacks
Stage 2 - Panic attacks
Stage 3 - Hypochondriasis
Stage 4 - Limited phobias
Stage 5 - Social phobias
Stage 6 - Extensive phobic avoidance/agoraphobia
Stage 7 - Depression

The disorder frequently starts with spontaneous subpanic attacks. These are one or two symptoms surging in isolation with little or no provocation. Examples include tachycardia, lightheadedness, and shortness of breath that occur without full panic attacks. In Stage 2, these symptoms are often accompanied by a flight or an immobilization ("freeze") response, and feelings of mental panic and loss of control.

Because the patients are in a high fear arousal state and parts of their body appear to race out of control for no immediately apparent reason, many fear their problem must be due to some serious medical illness. Interpretations that they are just anxious are often not reassuring since the experience of spontaneous panic attacks is so often beyond any prior stress or anxiety experience. At this stage they are frequently labeled hypochondriacal because of their repeated medical help-seeking behavior and their preoccupation with health (Stage 3).

Over time, spontaneous panic attacks occur in a wide variety of situations. Soon patients report that they avoid the situations associated with their most intense attacks, and they experience anticipatory anxiety on approaching those situations. They have limited phobic avoidance (Stage 4).

If the panic attacks persist, patients acquire more phobias and the existing phobias generalize. They become more socially phobic and eventually agoraphobic and polyphobic (Stages 5 and 6). The number and particular choice of phobia appear to be a function of the intensity, the chronicity, the frequency of the spontaneous panic attacks, and the situations in which they occurred.

Other factors may contribute to the genesis of the phobias, of course, and they may be reinforced in a variety of ways. With the progressive restrictions of the phobias, the increasing disability, the spread of anxiety and fear into every sector of their life, and with no relief, patients become progressively depressed (Stage 7).

A patient may be propelled rapidly through these stages in a short period of time if the panic attacks are intense and frequent. The patient may reach a certain stage and then the spontaneous panic attacks lessen or remit and the patient does not progress further through the stages of the anxiety disorder. The disorder may spontaneously remit for a time during which the patient emerges from the disorder. A recurrence of the panic attacks at a later time may propel the patient on to a different stage of the disorder.

Patients who have remissions and relapses move up and down through the stages over time. Those whose spontaneous panic attacks do not remit usually progress to the end stages of the disease. It is largely the relentless onslaught of frequent, intense, spontaneous panic attacks that dictates the rapidity and completeness of progression through the stages. Some of the stages, particularly Stage 3 (hypochondriasis) and Stage 7 (depression), may in certain cases present out of order from the natural sequence. Nonetheless, the majority progress from spontaneous attacks to progressive phobic avoidance behavior to increasing depression.

A cross-sectional evaluation leads the clinician to assign different diagnostic labels to each stage of the disorder and even to different symptoms within each stage. In contrast, the longitudinal perspective of the disorder as a single evolving process, rather than as several discrete entities, helps avoid this confusing fragmentation.

A Practical Diagnostic Strategy

The author finds the current classifications of anxiety and phobic disorders too complex, cumbersome, and clinically confusing to be useful. In addition they do not provide the best guide to the appropriate strategy. As a step toward a simpler, clearer, and more practical alternative classification to guide research efforts and clinical management, the approach outlined in Figure 6-1 is offered (6-8). Through a sequence of diagnostic steps, this decision tree guides the clinician to a diagnosis that predicts each patient's response to a specific treatment strategy. The treatment strategies for each of these diagnostic types is outlined later in this chapter. Because endogenous anxiety with or without phobias presents clinicians with the greatest diagnostic and therapeutic challenges, its treatment will be given more attention.

This classification proposes two kinds of anxiety disorder: exogenous and endogenous anxiety. The central differentiating question in the diagnosis is whether or not unexpected anxiety or unexpected symptom attacks have occurred. When severe, there may be intense polysymptomatic panic attacks with a flight response. When mild, these attacks are sudden, unexpected spikes of isolated symptoms above the ongoing drone of tension and anxiety. If these attacks have occurred during the natural history of the disorder, the patient is diagnosed as having endogenous anxiety.

The patient has exogenous anxiety if such attacks do not and never have occurred in the natural course of the disorder and if the anxiety is always clearly a response to an immediate environmental stress. Exogenous anxiety is like normal anxiety. It occurs only in response to a trauma or stress or is bound to one specific stimulus (e.g., a monophobia), but the symptoms do not occur in other circumstances. The symptoms never occur in unexpected surges. An exogenous anxiety is not diagnosed by the presence of psychological stressors, but rather is a residual category, based on the absence of spontaneous anxiety or spontaneous symptom attacks.

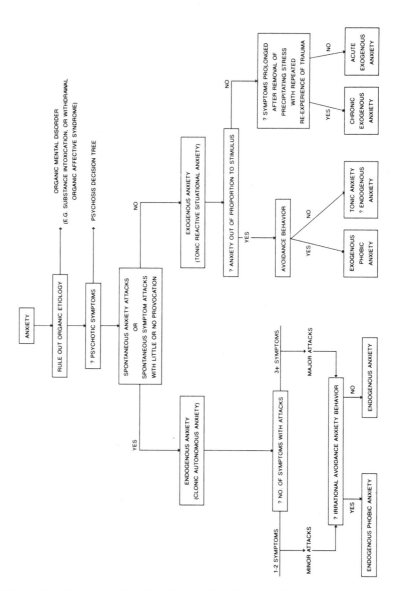

Figure 6-1. Decision Tree for Diagnosing Anxiety Disorders

Source: Sheehan DV and Sheehan KE, 1982-83. Reprinted with permission.

In contrast, endogenous anxiety is associated with multiple symptoms and usually with multiple phobias. The exogenous category is stress related or stimulus bound, whereas the evidence suggests that the endogenous category may be a genetically inherited metabolic disease. In contrast to the tonic quality of exogenous anxiety, endogenous anxiety is a spiky, clonic, phasic disorder that appears to be autonomous. The terms endogenous and exogenous are not intended to be used exclusively to evoke an etiology for each, as in depression. Rather they are used to describe the patient's experience at the moment of the attack. If the patient really believes that some of the attacks occur with little or no immediate, obvious, justifiable, external stress but seem to come from within and are autonomous, then descriptively the anxiety is of the endogenous variety.

These two major anxiety categories may be divided on the basis of severity and chronicity. When endogenous anxiety is chronic and severe, many phobias are likely to be present. Because the presence of phobias in addition to the spontaneous panic attacks calls for additional treatment intervention (behavior therapy) beyond the use of medication for the core panic attacks, endogenous phobic anxiety is regarded as a subtype of pure endogenous anxiety. Exogenous anxiety usually responds well to psychological or behavioral treatments. In contrast, endogenous anxiety usually requires drug treatment for optimal results (3,9).

Is there any evidence that supports this dichotomous classification? Preliminary evidence suggests that the age of onset distribution, sex ratio, and treatment response are different in the two kinds of anxiety (3,10-12).

It is unlikely that consensus on classification will be reached by clinicians or researchers based on symptom clustering alone. Indeed it would be unwise to accept any classification of these disorders (including Figure 6-1) as a final satisfactory solution. They are only more or less useful predictors that permit an economy of memory. The debate will undoubtedly continue until laboratory techniques for endogenous anxiety are developed such as special blood and urine tests, psychophysiological measurements, genetic marking, and pharmacological dissection.

Such ancillary diagnostic aids will lend validity to some

existing classification system and will suggest refinements that will be clinically meaningful. The classification in Figure 6-1 will undoubtedly be refined. But further useful subdivisions probably will be based on biological subtyping rather than clinical or symptom configuration. Some biological subtyping of endogenous anxiety that will more precisely predict treatment response, for example, will be a positive step in that direction. Until then, this diagnostic classification may offer a clearer starting point and simpler guide to correct diagnosis and treatment and to the future biological investigation of pathological anxiety.

Etiological Models of Anxiety

In science, models attempt to bring order and lucidity to the variety of observations. A good model is a description of events and especially their interplay that reflects reality accurately. A first step toward understanding and mastery, a model usually guides the direction of our research efforts, and helps us predict and perhaps learn to control the mechanisms of nature.

Historically, three models have been offered in attempts to understand anxiety:

1. The psychological or psychosocial model.
2. The behavioral model.
3. The biological model.

A fourth, medical model (for endogenous anxiety only) attempts to integrate these three models while reevaluating the relative contributions of each.

The psychological or psychosocial model proposes that all anxiety results from an interplay of environmental stresses and internal psychological conflicts (from the past and the present). The anxiety response is considered an attempt to mobilize and ward off overwhelming threat.

The behaviorists propose that anxiety can occur even in the absence of conflict. Following the principles of learning theory, anxiety response is believed to be acquired. It may be a classically conditioned response to trauma or an emitted behavior that has been reinforced by operant conditioning, or both.

Many physicians suggest that there is a physical basis for abnormal anxiety, that is, that abnormal anxiety is the manifestation of a medical disease to which there appears to be a genetic vulnerability. This biological model views abnormal anxiety as nature malfunctioning much as it does in other diseases such as diabetes mellitus or hypertension.

Each of these models, the environmental stress-psychological model, the behavioral model, and the biological model, has contributed something to our overall understanding of abnormal anxiety. But each tells only part of the story. A better model requires an integrated perspective accommodating the earlier models, while readjusting the relative importance of each and redefining their interplay.

The Medical Model

The medical model is an integrated one. It is a model for endogenous anxiety only; it does not relate to exogenous anxiety, in which psychological, social, and behavioral factors appear to predominate. The medical model of endogenous anxiety shown in Figure 6-2 proposes that the main contribution to this disorder is a genetic vulnerability to a biological disease state. This core biological vulnerability discharges symptoms in various parts of the body in an epileptiform fashion. There may be sudden spikes and rapid surges of anxiety for little or no obvious reason. These symptoms, which typically occur in clusters and at a rate of from two to five attacks per week, are often referred to as panic attacks. The condition usually first manifests itself in young women in their late teens or early twenties.

Over time these core biological attacks become associated with events in the environment that may themselves elicit symptoms. Eventually, the symptoms can be elicited and reinforced from within by the biological core disease as well as by environmental stimuli, following a learning theory model. In addition, the disorder itself often lasts for years, and if psychological or psychosocial factors are significant, they may aggravate the onset of the disorder and reinforce its severity and chronicity.

Apparently, the lower the genetic loading for the disorder,

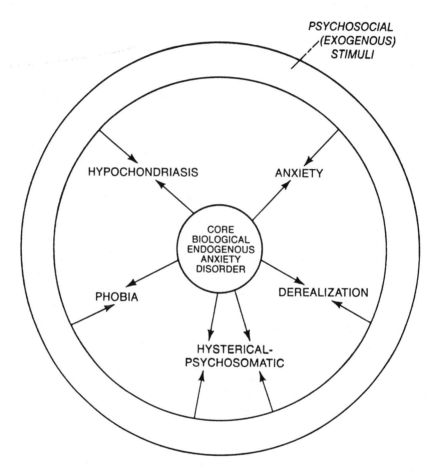

Figure 6-2. A Medical Model of Endogenous Anxiety

Source: Sheehan DV, et al., 1980. Reprinted with permission.

the greater the psychosocial stress required to activate and aggravate it. Conversely, those with a greater biological vulnerability to the disorder will require little or no stress to activate and maintain it, and the condition may appear quite autonomous. In the future, when the technology is available to measure the stress input and biological susceptibility to the disorder with greater percision, it may be possible to represent the severity and chronicity of the disorder as a differential equation that expresses the relative contributions of both. For example:

A (stress input) x B (biological susceptibility)
x C (conditioning) = Y (severity) x Z (chronicity).

The medical model attempts to integrate the three preexisting models. These models or forces are the threads connecting the stages described earlier. Understanding them helps explain the natural progression of the disorder and the interplay of the various symptoms and complications. Together with the longitudinal perspective of the disease passing through its several stages, these three forces and their interplay paint a richer picture of how the many parts may be woven together. Like all models in science the medical model will be improved and refined. In the meantime it offers a focus for research efforts and a framework for treatment strategy.

Treatment of Endogenous Anxiety

Treatment strategy is best formulated by first identifying its objectives. In the endogenous anxiety disease we can identify four treatment targets:

Target 1 - The biological core
Target 2 - The phobic behavior
Target 3 - The psychosocial aggravators and
            complications
Target 4 - Long-term management

Target 1 - Biological Core

The first and most important step in treating endogenous anxiety with or without its complicating phobias is to control the biological core of the disorder with antipanic medication. Although psychological treatments alone have been effective for some victims of the disorder, it is unclear if the response is better than one would expect from the spontaneous remission rate. Behavioral treatments, although effective in reducing phobic behavior in some patients, may not be effective against other sectors of the disorder (e.g., spontaneous panic attacks) and when used alone they may not be effective enough for the majority of these patients.

Several classes of drugs that have shown promise as effective antipanic drugs are the following:
1. Monoamine oxidase (MAO) inhibitors
2. Tricyclic antidepressants
3. The triazolo benzodiazepine, alprazolam
4. The triazolo pyridine, trazodone
5. The tetracyclic mianserin

The overall differences in efficacy among these drugs appears to be small. If used correctly, any one of them probably would be effective in the mild and early stages of the disorder. It is in the more severe and chronic cases that their differences and relative powers become more apparent.

Among the range of choices, alprazolam appears to be the least toxic and the most rapidly effective (13), although it appears to be a less potent antidepressant or mood elevator in these patients than the other drugs. Because of its speed of action and relative safety compared to the alternatives, I usually favor alprazolam as the first drug in the series to try in the majority of cases. However, the MAO inhibitor phenelzine is probably the single most effective drug overall. In severe and chronic cases, especially those complicated by considerable disability and depression, phenelzine is especially valuable.

Principles of Drug Treatment. In the past, antianxiety drugs have all too often been prescribed too casually and in subtherapeutic doses. Much time needs to be spent with the patient in reviewing regulation of doses, timing throughout the day, and in monitoring complications.

Several antipanic drugs require three to six weeks of treatment before significant benefit is achieved. Because the drugs are disruptive to take in these early weeks, the dose has to be increased gradually and it takes time, patience, and persistence to reach the final optimal dose for each patient. The best therapeutic effect usually is achieved at the dose where there is some sensation of regular persistent (but tolerable) side effects. The physician's efforts are directed to achieving the best balance between side effects and ideal benefit. This requires both clinical skill and careful monitoring.

Alprazolam (Xanax). With a starting dose of 0.5 mg three times daily, the total daily dose may be increased by 0.5 mg/day every two days. When the patient experiences either significant side effects (e.g., drowsiness) or benefit, no further dose increases are necessary. If the patient loses both significant side effects and the benefit, a further dose increase may be necessary. In the early weeks of treatment it is not unusual for the patient to pass through two or three such dose plateaus. However, it is not necessary to continue escalating the dose endlessly.

When the dose of 2 mg tid po is reached, further dose additions may be given at bedtime or taken at 4-5 hour intervals. Although the half-life of alprazolam is 10-12 hours, its duration of therapeutic action is a considerably shorter 4-5 hours. If doses are spaced too far apart, e.g., 8 hours, some recurrence of symptoms may be experienced. If the doses are taken with food, the drug is more slowly absorbed, the drowsiness and other side effects are less acute, and the antipanic effects last a little longer.

The average therapeutic dose at which antipanic benefit was achieved in our studies was 6 mg/day. There was, however, a considerable range of effective therapeutic doses—from 3 to 10 mg/day. Drowsiness, ataxia, and slurring of speech are the most apparent side effects at high doses. Episodic forgetfulness, increased assertiveness, irritability, and headaches are not uncommon at first, and some patients experience a depressed amotivational syndrome after several weeks.

Because alprazolam is also an anticonvulsant, it should never be abruptly or rapidly withdrawn, even when it is not effective, as this could lead to a withdrawal seizure. The best withdrawal schedule is to lower the dose at a rate of

1/2 to 1 mg every one to two weeks if an improved patient is attempting a drug-free trial. No matter what the circumstances, this author would not recommend withdrawal at a rate faster than 1 mg every three days. If good control of spontaneous anxiety attacks is not achieved by 10 mg/day after three to four weeks and/or the patient still has a significant depression, then the alprazolam trial should be considered a therapeutic failure.

Monoamine oxidase inhibitors. Both the hydrazine inhibitors—e.g., phenelzine (Nardil) and isocarboxazid (Marplan)—and the nonhydrazine MAOI tranylcypromine (Parnate) are effective in treating endogenous anxiety. However, the hydrazines, and particularly phenelzine, appear to be superior to tranylcypromine at optimal doses, especially in difficult cases (14,15).

Starting with 15 mg/day, phenelzine may be increased by 15 mg every four days. Thereafter the dose can be increased by 15 mg every week until some of the typical side effects appear. One of the most reliable guides to the best therapeutic dose is the dose at which the patient has some degree of postural hypotension as measured by the sphygmomanometer. With the patient both sitting and standing, the blood pressure is estimated at each visit. Close to the best therapeutic dose can be found when the blood pressure drops and recovers more slowly than normal at standing. At this level even small changes in dose can have a significant effect in bringing on both side effects and benefit. Consequently, very careful titration of the dose is necessary.

Several methods have some merit in minimizing the postural hypotension so frequent in the early stages of treatment. Taking the tablets at the end of meals (in which there is usually a small amount of tyramine), taking salt tablets, ensuring adequate hydration, and even adding 0.1 mg of Flourinef all have been helpful in certain cases in addition to decreasing the MAOI dose. Drinking colas, coffee, and tea may increase the blood pressure a little (but not excessively) and counteract the hypotensive and bradycardia effects of hydrazine MAO inhibitors.

Recent antipanic drugs. Although at this time there are no systematic studies documenting that trazodone or mianserin are effective for panic attacks and polyphobic behavior, we and others have found them to be useful in many cases, even in the absence of significant concomitant depression. At therapeutically effective doses these drugs are not without significant side effects. Trazodone appears to have a lower anticholinergic side effect profile than tricyclic antidepressants, although nasal congestion and sedation are not uncommon. Figure 6-3 is offered as a clinical guide to the relative benefits and side effects of the various antipanic drugs and may be of assistance in making a useful choice among the several options available.

Not all antidepressants are particularly helpful against panic attacks. For example, bupropion (16) and amoxapine are not predictably effective in endogenous anxiety.

Treating Resistant Cases. Those who are referred treatment-resistant cases frequently find themselves having to use amounts of all of the above effective drugs in doses that are in excess of the recommended levels (e.g., above 300 mg/day of a tricyclic or above 90 mg/day of phenelzine). If a patient derives no benefit and has no significant side effects at the maximum recommended dose, then further increases in the dose should be considered. It is often necessary to do this even when the tricyclic blood level or MAO platelet inhibition level suggest the dose may be adequate. The value of these lab tests may have been overestimated. Their role is ancillary and they are not intended as a substitute for clinical judgment and experience.

Length of Treatment. A therapeutic trial of these drugs should be considered a failure if adequate therapeutic benefit has not been achieved after three to four weeks on alprazolam or six to eight weeks on a good therapeutic dose of the remaining drugs shown in the treatment strategy in Figure 6-4. When therapeutic benefit is achieved, trials of 6-12 months are recommended. Over the months of treatment the dose may require further adjustments if either tolerance or troublesome side effects occur. When the drug is to be discontinued after several months of improvement, it is best done very slowly, preferably over several weeks. This helps minimize withdrawal and the danger of reactivating the disorder. The relapse rate is high.

Figure 6-3. Relative Merits and Disadvantages of Several Antipanic Drugs

* The author has had insufficient experience with trazodone to gauge this side effect.

Note: Numbers reflect the strength or likelihood of the drug's effects, on a ten-point scale, as compared with the others. If a specific side effect causes problems, use of an effective agent that is less likely to produce the effect may be helpful. Weights are based on the author's clinical experience and are offered as clinical guides rather than statements of scientific fact.

Source: Sheehan DV and Sheehan KE, 1982. Reprinted with permission.

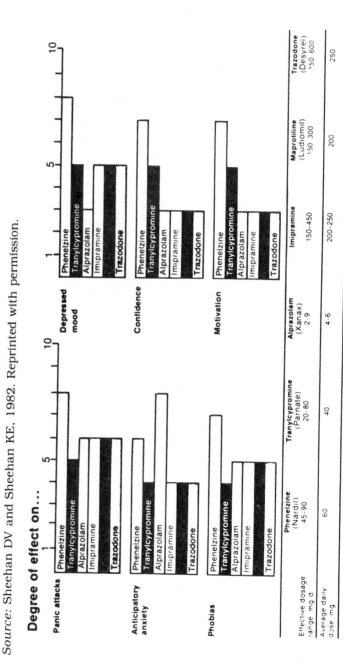

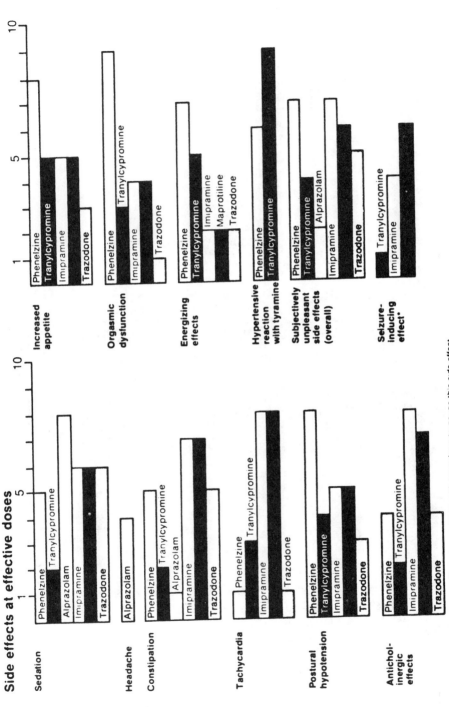

Side effects at effective doses

The author has had insufficient experience with trazodone to gauge this side effect

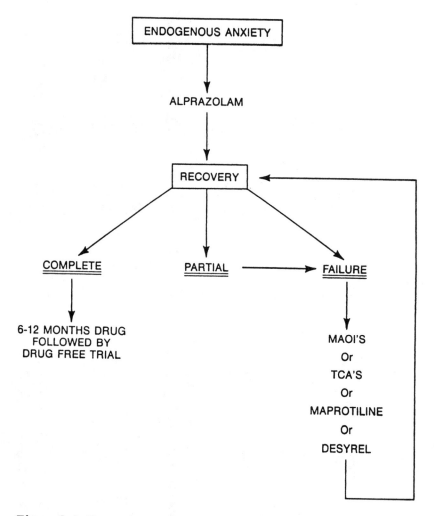

Figure 6-4. Management Strategy for Endogenous Anxiety
Source: Sheehan DV and Sheehan KE, 1982.

Target 2 - Phobic Behavior

If phobias complicate the core endogenous anxiety disorder (i.e., the patient has endogenous phobic anxiety), the treatment strategy in Figure 6-5 is followed. This is essentially the same treatment strategy for pure endogenous anxiety except that after the biological core spontaneous attacks are controlled with medication, behavior therapy (particularly exposure treatment) is used to extinguish any remaining phobias.

Sometimes the drugs alone control the spontaneous attacks and the phobic anxiety. This is particularly true when the disorder is milder and more recent in onset. If the panic attacks are severe and chronic, the phobic avoidance behavior is more ingrained. In such cases some phobic behavior usually persists after the core panic attacks are controlled by medication. The active ingredient of many behavior therapies for phobias is said to be the amount of real life exposure to the phobic stimulus (17,18). There is usually good extinction of the phobic avoidance behavior when this exposure is intense, lasts for a long time (two to three hours), is repeatedly practiced, and the usual avoidance response is prevented. The operating principle here is direct action rather than too much discussion. The clinician who brings his phobic patient directly into the phobic situation and enlists the help of family and friends in repeatedly practicing the exposure will get better phobic extinction than the clinician who spends long hours discussing the ramifications of the phobia with the patient.

Target 3 - Psychological Target

Older models of this disorder held that patients with panic attacks and multiple phobias must be overreacting to psychosocial problems or an unconscious conflict. Whereas psychosocial factors are sometimes important as aggravators in the onset and maintenance of these symptoms, they are by no means always present or even relevant to the disorder. When they are present and complicate recovery, psychotherapy is indicated. But is should not be imposed on those who do not feel psychosocial factors are important in their condition.

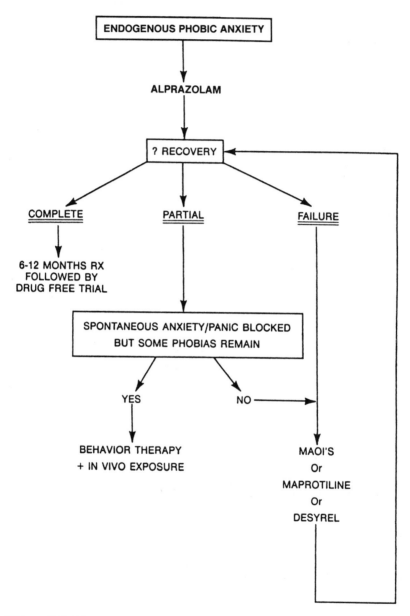

Figure 6-5. Management Strategy for Endogenous Phobic Anxiety
Source: Sheehan DV and Sheehan KE, 1982.

When the panic attacks have been controlled with medication and the phobias extinguished with behavior therapy, any remaining psychosocial problems will come into sharper focus. At this point the patient feels more motivated and capable of dealing with them and usually sees the issues more clearly.

Target 4 - Long-Term Management

Because this disorder is chronic and disabling in the majority of cases, patients require special long-term care. Many suffer relapses after the medication treatment is stopped. The goal of long-term management is to prevent relapses or to treat them as early as possible and to maintain the gains achieved with the first three targets of treatment. It may be important to identify the relapse aggravators for each patient. These are not always psychosocial but may result from drinking alcohol, smoking marijuana, being medically ill, being in the premenstrual phase of the cycle, or being careless in taking medication.

Each patient may have individual warning signs of a relapse. For example, a typical sequence involves first the onset of headaches that persist and are refractory to aspirin, then little subpanic symptom attacks, and an increase in depression followed within two weeks by a full-blown panic attack. Left untreated the disorder then progresses through the stages in its natural history outlined earlier. Over time there is progressive phobic avoidance behavior and increasing depression. Watching such relapses occur when the patient is reluctant to restart medication offers an opportunity to study the natural history of the disorder as it deteriorates.

Treatment of Exogenous Anxiety

An exogenous anxiety or phobia requires a different treatment strategy than does the endogenous variety (Figure 6-6). For an exogenous phobia that occurs in the absence of any spontaneous attacks, behavior therapy and particularly exposure treatment is the intervention of choice. If the exposure is done in a graduated way, it is less frightening.

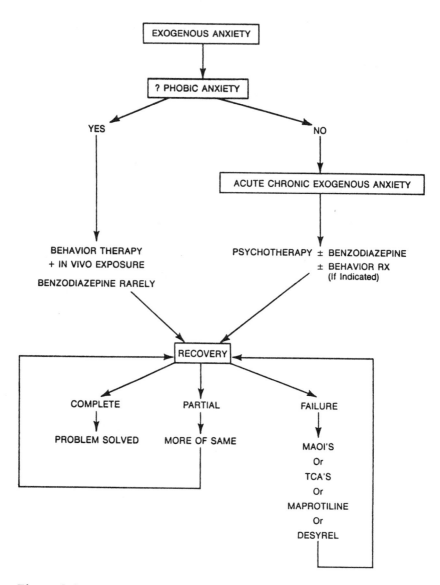

Figure 6-6. Management Strategy and Exogenous Anxiety
Source: Sheehan DV and Sheehan KE, 1982.

Exposure sessions of 1-1/2 to 3 hours are much more valuable than shorter exposure periods. Real life exposure is considerably superior to imaginal exposure; if a patient fears dogs or insects, introducing real dogs or insects into the treatment setting should be planned. In these cases tranquilizers are rarely indicated. However, if after our best efforts the patient fails to improve after three months or 12 sessions using this approach, a trial of one of the drugs discussed earlier for endogenous anxiety may be necessary. Although the patient may appear to have a single exogenous phobia, he or she may indeed have a low grade or early phase of endogenous anxiety. The in vivo exposure is repeated after the medication has been regulated. At this point, rapid extinction usually occurs with exposure where it had failed to do so before.

With acute or chronic exogenous anxiety it is necessary to identify the psychosocial factors that precipitated or maintain the symptoms. Psychotherapy is the treatment of choice for this problem. It helps to clarify the problems, to review possible solutions in dealing with them, and to provide the necessary framework of support for the patient to make any changes that are required to work them through. As with the exogenous phobia, medication is rarely necessary in these cases. However, if the best psychotherapeutic efforts fail within a reasonable period of time, then the various antipanic drugs may be considered. Fortunately this is necessary only in a minority of such cases.

Conclusion

The 1980s have brought a renewed interest in pathological anxiety. These research efforts will lead us closer to a more precise understanding and better control over this crippling disease. In the meantime it is hoped that the strategies and framework offered here will help clinicians in their efforts to bring relief to the lives of these frightened people.

References

1. American Psychiatric Association: Diagnostic and Statistical Manual of Mental Disorders, 3rd ed. Washington, DC, American Psychiatric Association, 1980

2. Sokal RR, Sneath PH: Principles of Numerical Taxonomy. San Francisco, W.H. Freeman and Co., 1963

3. Sheehan DV, Ballenger J, Jacobson G: The treatment of endogenous anxiety with phobic, hysterical and hypochondriacal symptoms. Arch Gen Psychiatry 37:51-59, 1980

4. Feighner JP, Robins E, Guze SB, Woodruff RA, Winokur G, Munoz R: Diagnostic criteria for use in psychiatric research. Arch Gen Psychiatry 26:57-63, 1972

5. Spitzer RL, Endicott J, Robins E: Research Diagnostic Criteria (RDC) for a Selected Group of Functional Disorders, 2nd ed. Biometrics Research, Instrument 58. New York State Psychiatric Institute, Nov 23, 1975

6. Sheehan DV, Sheehan KE: The classification of anxiety and hysterical states, part I: historical review of empirical delineation. J Clin Psychopharmacology 2:235-244, 1982

7. Sheehan DV, Sheehan KE: The classification of phobic disorders. Int J Psychiatry Med 12:243-264, 1982-83

8. Sheehan DV, Sheehan KE: The classification of anxiety and hysterical states, part II: towards a more heuristic classification. J Clin Psychopharmacology 2:286-393, 1982

9. Klein DF, Rabkin JG, eds: Anxiety: New Research and Changing Concepts. Raven Press, New York, 1981

10. Sheehan DV: Panic and phobic disorders. New Engl J Med 307:156-158, 1982

11. Carey G, Gottesman I: Twin and family studies of anxiety, phobic and obsessive disorders, in Anxiety: New Research and Changing Concepts. Edited by Klein DF, Rabkin JG. New York, Raven Press, 1981

12. Sheehan DV, Sheehan KE, Minichiello WE: Age of onset of phobic disorders: a reevaluation. Compr Psychiatry 22:544-553, 1981

13. Sheehan DV, Coleman JH, Greenblatt DJ: Some biochemical correlates of agoraphobia with panic attacks and their response to a new treatment. J Clinical Psychopharmacology, 1984 (in press)

14. Sheehan DV, Claycomb JB, Kouretas N: Monoamine oxidase inhibitors: prescription and patient management. Int J Psychiatry Med 10:99-121, 1980

15. Sheehan DV, Claycomb JB: The use of MAO inhibitors in clinical practice, in Psychiatric Medicine Update: Mass. General Hospital Review for Physicians. Edited by Manschreck TC. New York, Elsevier, 1983

16. Sheehan DV, Davidson J, Manschreck TC, Van Wyck Fleet J: Lack of efficacy of a new antidepressant (Bupropion) in the treatment of panic disorder with phobias. J Clin Psychopharmacol 3:23-31, 1983

17. Marks IM: The current status of behavioral psychotherapy: theory and practice. Am J Psychiatry 133:253-261, 1966

18. Sherman AR: Real life exposure as a primary therapeutic factor in the desensitisation treatment of fear. J Abnorm Psychol 79:19-28, 1972

Behavioral Approaches to the Evaluation and Treatment of Anxiety Disorders

Richard L. Heinrich, M.D.

7

Behavioral Approaches to the Evaluation and Treatment of Anxiety Disorders

Richard L. Heinrich, M.D.

Introduction

Mrs. Smith* is a 24-year-old, married commercial artist who works for a large corporation and has to fly frequently as part of her job. She is seeking help with an increasing fear of flying that is interfering with her work.

Dr. Jason is a 28-year-old, recently married resident in internal medicine who has been experiencing a variety of unexplained symptoms including palpitations, insomnia, muscle tension, and frequent diaphoreses. He also notes that he has become increasingly concerned about his ability to function as a physician.

Mrs. Alexis was three-months pregnant when ruminative thoughts of harming her baby led her current therapist to refer her for "behavior therapy." Prior to the patient's pregnancy she had been treated with supportive psychotherapy and antipsychotic medications for fears and anxieties associated with her recent move from the East Coast.

---

*All patients' names have been changed.

Mr. Catalona is a 40-year-old manager who has had to take a leave of absence from his firm because of unexplained pain. He was recently admitted to the hospital's psychiatry service because of a suicide attempt. His wife reports that over a six-month period he was becoming more and more fearful and depressed and was unable to be alone for any length of time or to leave their house.

Each of these individuals is experiencing an anxiety disorder. As Dr. Pasnau indicated in Chapter 1, these disorders are not uncommon. Physicians and mental health professionals are often called upon to help people with these types of problems. The first patient, Mrs. Smith, was later diagnosed as having a phobic disorder. The second patient, Dr. Jason, was eventually diagnosed as having an adjustment disorder with anxious mood. The third patient, Mrs. Alexis, was diagnosed as having an obsessive-compulsive disorder. The fourth patient, Mr. Catalona, was diagnosed as having panic disorder with agoraphobia. In each of these four and the other anxiety disorders that constitute the third edition of the *Diagnostic and Statistical Manual of Mental Disorders* (DSM-III) nosology of anxiety disorders, mentioned in Chapter 1, behavioral principles and approaches are playing greater role in evaluation and therapy.

This chapter highlights the principles of learning that are central to a behavioral understanding of anxiety disorders and presents an overview of behavioral assessment techniques and treatment approaches that psychiatrists and mental health professionals can use in their practices.

Learning Principles

The major theme that informs a behavioral understanding of anxiety disorders as well as normal behavior is the central role of learning in each. Learning theorists assume that principles of normal development and behavior apply equally to the development and maintenance of abnormal behavior (1). As Marks argues in his book, *Cure and Care of the Neuroses*, this assumption has not yet been adequately researched and demonstrated (2). Nonetheless, the learning theory model has enough support to provide the researcher and clinician with a useful working hypothesis regarding the development and maintenance of the various anxiety disorders.

Animal studies have been used to illustrate how different types of learning such as classical conditioning, operant conditioning, and social learning may operate in the development of phobic and obsessive-compulsive disorders (3-6). In a series of studies with rats, Miller was able to condition fear responses to experimental cages that were painted white. Each time the rats were put into the white side of the experimental cage they were electrically shocked. They were also trained to escape from the white side of the cage by turning a wheel that led to another compartment. The rats acquired the fear response and maintained it whenever placed in a white environment, even when they were no longer in danger of receiving a shock. These fear responses were very difficult to extinguish because the animal rarely tested the consequences of remaining in the white cage; if an escape was available, the rats would try to remove themselves as quickly as possible. This failure to test the consequences of behavior and the risks that are involved in trying a new behavior (giving up ritualistic and avoidant behaviors) may suggest why patients with anxiety disorders are so difficult to treat by conventional therapies.

These experiments led to further research by Miller, Masserman, Seligman, and others that illustrates the potential role of learning in the formation of phobias and ritualistic behavior (3-6). In clinical presentations, learning principles which may be operating can be elicited by a careful history.

> For example, Mrs. Smith reported that she had enjoyed flying until two years prior to seeking treatment. At that time she had to go on a business trip shortly after a major airline crash occurred (pairing a negative stimulus with a previously neutral or, in this situation, positive event). On subsequent flying trips she noted increasing anxiety, especially on takeoffs and landings and in turbulence (stimulus generalization). Eventually she began noticing extreme anxiety when she was told that she would have to fly, on the night before going to the airport, and during the drive to the airport (anticipatory anxiety).

Characteristics of Behavioral Assessment

Both the experimental method and the learning theory origins of behavioral therapy have left their marks on the process of assessment (1,7). Similar to a scientist engaged in research, the behaviorally oriented clinician proceeds in a systematic manner with established protocols. The general outline of the protocols include: (a) an immediate, direct focus on the presenting symptom or problem; (b) operationally defining various parameters of the problem; (c) collecting baseline information; (d) setting treatment goals; and (e) teaching the patient new behaviors or skills that will effectively resolve the presenting problems.

As part of this scientific legacy, the behavior therapy techniques that are used to teach new behaviors to patients are based on empirical research. In addition, because assessment is an integral part of *each* stage of treatment, this commitment to evaluation is a major ingredient of the treatment of each individual (8).

Although behavior therapists have contended that this commitment to the experimental approach makes behavior therapy unique and sets it apart from the "medical model" and traditional psychoanalytic and psychodynamic therapies (1), the overlap between behavior therapy and other approaches is significant. In fact, proponents of a medical model would also emphasize the need for experimental methods and would empirically evaluate various treatment approaches.

Perhaps the unique aspect of the behavioral approach is the focus on behavior per se and the conditions that maintain the problem. Unlike biological or psychoanalytical and psychodynamic approaches in which the complaints of anxiety are considered to represent underlying disordered physiology or psychopathology, the behavioral approach regards the presenting anxiety complaint as the major focus of evaluation and treatment. This unique focus is clearly delineated in the ongoing evaluation of the target symptom or behavior.

Formal Evaluation:
The Functional Assessment of Behavior

Although assessment continues throughout the treatment, a formal assessment precedes the initiation of the treatment phase. The assessment phase is designed to educate and prepare both the patient and the clinician for the treatment phase. During this phase the parameters of the presenting problem are defined. This assessment then provides the clinician with the necessary information to select appropriate treatment techniques.

Figure 7-1 outlines the process of a typical behavioral assessment. As in other models of assessment, the clinician begins by identifying problems (the presenting symptom or target behavior) and proceeds by formulating ther-

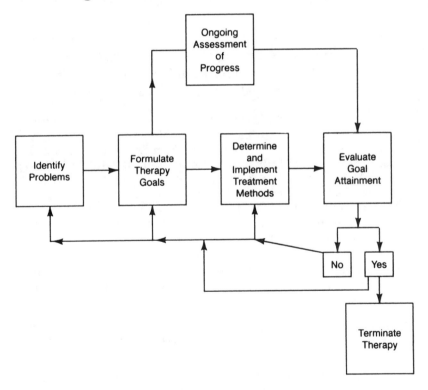

Figure 7-1. Treatment Evaluation and Behavior Therapy

Source: Taylor et al., 1982. Reprinted with permission.

apy goals, determining and implementing treatment methods, and evaluating goal attainment. This process begins by establishing a baseline of operationally defined behaviors and goals that are measured before treatment is initiated and then continued throughout the treatment program. An important outcome of this process is that patients are educated to become their own therapists and are given major responsibility throughout the initial evaluation and treatment phases.

The formal assessment phase begins with a functional analysis of behavior (8-11) that focuses on the relationships between the presenting symptoms or problems and the contexts in which they occur. A simple way to remember the functional analysis of behavior is the mnemonic A-B-C, in which A represents antecedents, B behaviors, and C consequences.

Antecedents (A) refer to any stimuli that precede the occurrence of the presenting complaint or target behavior. They can include interpersonal events, situations, thoughts, feelings, sensations, and behaviors.

> Dr. Jason noticed that when he woke up in the morning his anxiety would occur as soon as he thought about going to work. Mrs. Smith's anxiety would begin as soon as her boss would tell her about the next assignment requiring her to fly. Mrs. Alexis noted that her ruminative thoughts would increase after an unpleasant interaction with her mother or a fight with her husband. Mr. Catalona noted that as soon as he thought about going out of the house his breathing and heart rate would increase.

For each of these patients, thoughts, interpersonal events, or anticipated situations were the critical antecedent stimuli that could elicit their symptoms and problems.

Behaviors (B) refer to the overt and covert activities and experiences of individuals that make up human behavior. They can include thoughts, feelings, sensations, imagery, and interpersonal responses. Patients often come to psychiatrists because these behaviors are no longer under voluntary control, are experienced as disturbing, or impair their ability to function socially and/or vocationally. These behaviors thus become symptoms to be treated.

Mrs. Smith's terror of flying led her to seek therapy and to consider changing her job if she could not overcome her fear. Dr. Jason's physiological arousal and emotions were impairing his ability to work to the extent that he was thinking of dropping out of medicine altogether. Mrs. Alexis' ruminative thoughts made her wonder if she were going crazy. At times she thought of ending her life because the disturbing thoughts would not leave her mind. Mr. Catalona's marriage was severely strained and he lost his job because he couldn't leave his house by himself.

Each of these patients' behavior had become a symptom and was experienced as out of their control and seriously impairing their lives.

Consequences (C) are defined as what happens after the symptomatic behavior occurs. Even though patients may experience symptoms as disturbing and undesirable, significant positive, immediate, short-term consequences or reinforcement of their problems may occur. For example, they may receive attention and support from family members because of their problem.

Mrs. Alexis, who had to quit work as her pregnancy progressed, received increased attention from her mother and husband (positive reinforcement) because of her ruminative thoughts.

Patients may avoid unpleasant responsibilities such as a stressful job or a demanding spouse because of their symptoms.

Because of his symptoms, Mr. Catalona was able to avoid not only a job he did not like, but he also avoided his wife's sexual demands, which he found anxiety provoking.

In the first few interviews with a new client, these consequences may not be readily apparent. The clinician beginning with a new patient may be in a position similar to a stranger walking into Dr. Miller's research laboratory at the end of a fear-conditioning experiment and attempting to understand the rat's behavior. Without knowing the learning history, the animal's fear response to white cages would be unintelligible. Understanding the learning history provides a meaningful context for the animal's behavior. It explains that the persistent wheel turning is an attempt to escape the consequences of an unexpected shock even though no danger presently exists. Similarly, the clinician needs to discover from the patient and other sources the likely outcome if the patient's symptoms *did not* occur; e.g., returning to a stressful work situation or confronting a failing marriage. But the A-B-C method is only one approach to comprehensive behavioral assessment.

Kanfer and Saslow published a more detailed and comprehensive assessment scheme. They outlined seven domains that should be addressed:
1. Analysis of the problem situation (including behavioral excesses, deficits, and assets).
2. Clarification of the problem situation that maintains the targeted behaviors.
3. A motivational analysis.
4. A developmental analysis (including biological, sociological, and behavioral changes).
5. A self-control analysis.
6. Analysis of social relationships.
7. Analysis of the social, cultural, and physical environments (12).

Particularly noteworthy in this model is the emphasis on the assets of the individual as well as the formulation of problems in terms of excesses and deficits. The behavior therapist builds the treatment intervention on the assets of patients and focuses more on what they are able to do rather than what they are unable to do. The therapist also translates a problem into excesses or deficits. Conceptualized in this way, an anxiety disorder becomes an excess of dysfunctional thoughts and feelings and a deficit of skills that reduce the effects of stress and effectively respond to interpersonal situations. In anxiety disorders, excesses and deficits coexist and feed upon each other in a vicious cycle.

> Mrs. Smith's flying phobia, which could be conceptualized as an excessive fear response, was complicated by a lack of assertiveness with her boss. Her boss would frequently have her paged during her lunch hour to give her an assignment. She never told him that she did not want to be disturbed on

her lunch hour, nor did she ever request to postpone a trip because of her personal needs. An early part of the therapy program directed the patient to tell her boss that she did not want to be paged on her lunch hour and that she did not want to take any flying assignments for at least two months so that she could have treatment for her phobic disorder.

Obtaining Information: Assessment Methods

As with other approaches to assessment, the behavior therapist begins with an interview to establish therapeutic rapport to educate the patient and to elicit the A-B-C's of the presenting problem. To establish baselines, the behavioral interview and history moves from the general to the specific. Questions that guide the elicitation of information from the patient are: Where? When? With whom? How frequently? How long does it last? and How intense is it? Because many patients are not good observers of their behavior, role playing techniques can be helpful in obtaining information about the patient's abilities and deficits (13). Whenever possible, the reports of significant others about the patient's behavior in specific situations should be sought.

Because of the problems associated with retrospective reports and the clinical interview, standardized evaluation techniques and prospective assessments play a central role in the evaluation process (14,15). Self-report survey instruments and self-monitoring are particularly useful in anxiety disorders. One of the first survey instruments developed for the evaluation of phobias was Wolpe's Fear Survey Schedule. This is a questionnaire on which the patient rates the intensity of fears in diverse situations (16).

A variety of newer instruments now are available to assess important areas that may be associated with anxiety problems. Some of these instruments are the Behavioral Analysis History Questionnaire, the Reinforcement Survey Schedule, the Assertive Behavior Survey Schedule, and the Thought Stopping Survey Schedule (17). These instruments may give the clinician an important overview of the patient's functioning and may serve to pinpoint specific problem situations that patients may not report in the initial interviews.

Self-monitoring is a frequently employed assessment technique that is used by behavioral clinicians in the early phases of therapy. Behavioral diaries such as the one in Figure 7-2 are a form of self-monitoring that fulfills a variety of functions. In addition to providing useful, current information on the patient's problem and giving the patient a major role in the treatment process, the self-monitoring shifts the focus of the patient from symptoms to the situations that elicit or are incompatible with the symptoms. Instead of focusing on "why is this happening to me?" the patient learns to focus on "how" and "when" it happens. Another important function of the diaries is to assess how cooperative and compliant the patient will be with future homework assignments. Because behavior therapy requires that the patient assume major responsibility in the treatment process, it is important to identify noncompliance prior to initiating a treatment program.

In addition to diaries, mechanical devices such as wrist counters are occasionally used to keep track of specific target symptoms.

> Mrs. Alexis was asked to wear a wrist counter for two weeks and to count the number of "negative thoughts" (hurting her baby and hurting her husband) that occurred each day. She recorded this total number in a behavioral diary, thereby establishing a baseline frequency count prior to initiating treatment.

Two other methods of collecting information frequently employed in behavioral assessment are behavioral observation and psychophysiological measurement (18-20).

Behavioral observation is the most difficult to do in an office practice. However, with the advances in video technology it may be possible to have patients record themselves in home settings. Audio recordings are readily available to obtain "real time" behavior of patients. When the problem behaviors and symptoms occur in the home setting, the patient may be asked to audiotape at those times when it is likely for the anxiety problem to occur. If the problem has discrete parameters and is situation specific, the therapist or another trained observer can accompany

Target Symptom: _____

Name: _____

SYMPTOM DIARY

Date: _____

TIME	INTENSITY (0-100)	SITUATION Describe where you were	BEHAVIOR What were you doing?	THOUGHT/FEELINGS What were you thinking?

Figure 7-2. Symptom Diary. A behavioral diary kept by each patient plays an important role in shifting patient awareness from symptoms to situations.

the patient to the situation in which the problem occurs and observe their responses, e.g., going into an elevator or driving on the freeway. Spouses and other family members can also be used as observers if the target behavior is discrete and easy to rate, such as hours outside of the house or distance walked from the house. For inpatient settings, more sophisticated observation scales are available (21).

When these options are not available, role playing provides a method of simulating situations that may be influencing the patient's anxiety disorder.

> When the therapist engaged Mrs. Smith in a role play situation of how she responded to her boss on the telephone, it was clear that she had major assertive deficits that were not apparent from her behavior during therapy sessions.

Psychophysiological measures—electromyography, electrodermography, temperature, heart rate, and blood pressure—have played a prominent role in behavioral assessment and therapy. The recent preeminence of these measures is due to the popularity of biofeedback and the developing area of behavioral medicine (20,22). Psychophysiological measures may be useful in the evaluation and treatment phases of anxiety disorders. Inexpensive portable biofeedback devices can be used during the evaluation phase to assess levels of physiological arousal as patients describe or imagine various situations that elicit their anxiety disorder. A printout of this information provides both patient and therapist with a baseline record of arousal responses that can be used during treatment to evaluate the success of the intervention.

Although the psychophysiological measures often are regarded as more scientific and objective than the subjective self-report and self-monitoring measures, a number of investigators have noted the lack of concordance among cognitive, behavioral, and physiological measures of anxiety (23). In fact, some patients may demonstrate dramatic improvements in cognitive and behavioral functioning, e.g., returning to work and social life, yet still have physiological arousal responses to the situations that brought them into therapy (23). This lack of concordance highlights the need to choose evaluation measures that are appropriate to the specific problem and that provide meaningful outcomes to the patient.

Obtaining Information: Baselines

Because of behavior therapy's commitment to ongoing evaluation, a major goal of the behavioral assessment is the establishment of a baseline for the target behaviors that are to be treated. Baselines refer to the process of documenting the frequency and intensity of the target symptoms and behaviors before treatment is initiated.

Figure 7-3 is the result of Mrs. Alexis' recording of the number of negative thoughts she had per day using a wrist counter. During the week of self-monitoring, her negative thoughts began to decrease in frequency prior to any intervention. This probably is due to the reactive effects of self-monitoring, where the target behavior moves in the desired direction prior to beginning formal treatment. If such effects occur, the patient is instructed to continue the self-monitoring until a stable baseline is achieved or the problem extinguishes.

Figure 7-4 illustrates baselines that were obtained from Mrs. Smith, who was asked to describe the situations associated with flying that caused her distress. She then was directed to rate her distress in each scene with SUDS units (subjective units of distress scale) ranging from 0 to 100. Zero equals no distress at all and 100 equals the maximum amount of distress that one could withstand for only a few minutes. Notice that Mrs. Smith's distress does not increase in a linear fashion from one situation to the next. Certain scenes, one and four in particular—being told that she will have to fly and turbulence in the airplane—are rated as the most distressing. In the treatment phase, these scenes are rearranged to form a hierarchy of least distressing to most distressing.

Dr. Jason kept a daily and hourly record of his anxiety; the daily record is presented in Figure 7-5. It was clear from the daily baseline charting of Dr. Jason's anxiety that he experienced minimal anxiety on weekends and that over the course of the week his anxiety diminished, suggesting that most of his anxiety was work related.

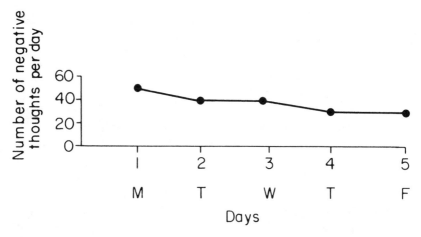

Figure 7-3. Five-day Pretreatment baseline for Mrs. Alexis's negative thoughts.

Note: Note the decrease in frequency associated with the self-monitoring alone in the absence of any other behavioral intervention.

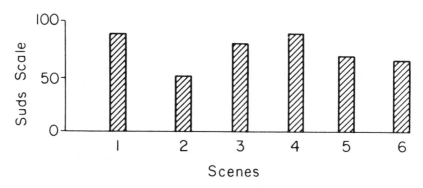

Figure 7-4. Mrs. Smith's subjective distress at imagining scenes related to her fear of flying.

Note: Scene 1—Receipt of assignment from boss
Scene 2—Drive to airport
Scene 3—Entering the plane
Scene 4—Takeoff
Scene 5—Turbulence
Scene 6—Landing
Note that scenes 1 and 4 are most distressing, and that distress does not build up in a linear fashion.

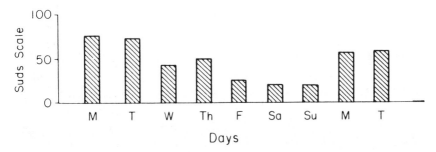

Figure 7-5. Dr. Jason's self-monitoring of anxiety on an hourly basis (pre-treatment), and totaled daily for nine days shows his greatest distress is experienced on Mondays and Tuesdays, with some relief on the weekend.

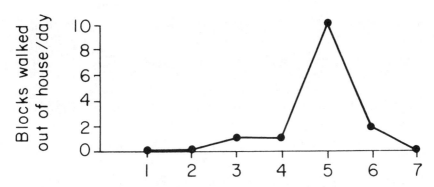

Figure 7-6. Graph of the number of blocks walked each day reveals that Mr. Catalona is virtually homebound.

Note: On day 5 Mr. Catalona walked to his therapy session accompanied by his wife.

Figure 7-6 shows Mr. Catalona's graph of the number of blocks he walked outside of his house each day. It's clear from his self-monitoring that he is virtually housebound. The only day that he walked out of the house was on day five when he attended his therapy session accompanied by his wife.

These four graphs are examples of baselines that clinicians and patients can establish with relative ease. They provide important information for treatment planning, they educate patients about the circumstances that make their problem better or worse, and in some cases they actually have a therapeutic effect (as in the case of Mrs. Alexis). They also set the stage for the treatment.

Behavioral Therapies

The Exposure Principle

Over the past 30 years there has been a virtual explosion of behavioral therapy approaches for psychiatric problems and, specifically, anxiety disorders (2). Table 7-1 summarizes some of the many techniques and interventions that have been developed to treat anxiety disorders.

What do these many techniques, so apparently diverse, have in common that unites them under the rubric of behavior therapy? The common unifying principle operating in all of the various treatment approaches listed in Table 7-1 is exposure to the feared stimulus during the course of treatment.

Marks presents the treatment of a ladder-climbing phobia to illustrate how the exposure principle operates in different treatment approaches (2). Relaxing in a chair and imagining climbing up the first rung of the ladder would be the beginning of a systematic densitization procedure. Climbing the first rung of the ladder in real life while staying relaxed would be the beginning of systematic desensitization in vivo. Climbing the ladder without the relaxation would be cognitive rehearsal, in vivo facilitation,

Table 7-1. Exposure Terms

Counterphobic treatment	Group confrontation
Prolonged exposure	Flooding
Exposure in vivo, in fantasy	Implosion
Arugamama	Massed practice
Paradoxical intention	High intensity stimulation
Participation	Reactive inhibition
Participant modeling	Catharsis
Contact desensitization	Programmed fantasy
Cognitive desensitization	Covert reinforcement
Desensitization in fantasy, in vivo	Emotional training
Systematic desensitization	Induced anxiety
Counterconditioning	Guided fantasy, imagining, daydreaming
Graduated extinction	Initiated symbol projection
Self-observation	Release therapy
Exposure homework	Acoustic mirror
Shaping	Stress inoculation, immunization
Reinforced practice	Anxiety management training
Successive approximation	Cognitive modification, insight
Respiratory relief	Cognitive restructuring
Aversion relief	Self-instruction
Deconditioning	Functional CS exposure

Source: Marks IM: Living With Fear, New York, McGraw-Hill, 1978. Reprinted with permission.

graded exposure, or behavioral rehearsal. Whether reinforcing the patient for climbing a step, grabbing the patient and placing him or her on the top of the ladder until the anxiety extinguishes, or teaching the patient an internal dialogue to repeat while climbing the ladder, all of these approaches expose the patient to the situation that evokes the anxiety or avoidance behavior until it no longer has the power to do so.

Mr. Catalona's avoidance behaviors had increased to the point of rarely leaving the house except for therapy sessions (see Figure 7-6). His wife decided that she no longer wanted to live with him and she left for another man. The patient became suicidal and was admitted to the hospital. During the first week of hospitalization it was noted that he rarely left the ward and frequently refused to go to the patients' cafeteria for meals. The patient was placed on imipramine with some initial improvement, but it was not sustained.

One of Mr. Catalona's primary fears was being in a crowded room. The patient's therapist began a program of gradual exposure to situations off the ward that evoked fear responses: going to the cafeteria, going to the gift shop, going to the gymnasium, and going to his work assignment. Within three to four weeks of graded exposure to these various situations the patient was able to go unaccompanied to his work assignment, to the gym, and to the cafeteria.

The major treatment approach with Mr. Catalona, as an inpatient and then as an outpatient, was exposure to the many evoking stimuli that ultimately had led to his agoraphobia and panic attacks.

Exposure Treatments: Systematic Desensitization, Implosion, and Flooding

Probably the best known behavioral treatment techniques are the "first generation," narrowly focused behavioral interventions such as systematic desensitization (4,24), implosion, and flooding (25). Systematic desensitization was developed by Wolpe, guided by the principle of counterconditioning. Wolpe reasoned that if animals could be conditioned with electric shock to have fear responses to a specific cage, then they could be counterconditioned by placing the animals in similar cages and by pairing that placement with a positive stimulus. Eventually such conditioning would lead to a neutral response to the original experimental cage that elicited a fear response. Similarly, pairing deep muscle relaxation with imagined situations that evoke fear in humans (graded exposure) should eventually countercondition the anxiety response in real life (reciprocal inhibition and extinction through desensitization).

The typical desensitization procedure begins with the therapist eliciting a description of the situations or scenes that are related to the specific problem presented by the patient.

Mrs. Smith described six different scenes that were related to her flying phobia: (1) being told by her boss that she would have to fly as part of an assignment, (2) driving to the airport, (3) entering the plane, (4) taking off, (5) turbulence during the flight, and (6) landing.

The patient is then instructed by the therapist to rate how much distress he or she experiences in each of the scenes on a distress scale such as the SUDS (0 to 100). Scenes are then rank ordered in a hierarchy from least distressing to most distressing (Figure 7-4).

During several sessions the patient is taught a relaxation technique, most often Jacobson's progressive muscle relaxation (26). Then, during the treatment sessions, the increasingly distressing scenes in the hierarchy are presented to the patient while he or she is deeply relaxed. This process continues until all of the scenes can be presented without evoking an anxiety response.

> Mrs. Smith had an excellent response to progressive muscle relaxation and was able to proceed through her hierarchy within eight sessions. After her eighth session and prior to taking her first flight, she arranged a guided tour of the airport and an airplane so that she could ask questions about the meaning and significance of turbulence, the process of landing, and so on. After the visit to the airport she then arranged to take a short flight (50 minutes) as her first step. On arrival at the airport she called her therapist (as had been arranged) to report any anxiety responses to the flight as well as to plan a strategy for the return flight. The patient reported no problems with either flight. At her six-month follow-up evaluation the patient was able to fly long distances without any recurrence of her anxiety responses.
>
> In addition to the systematic desensitization procedure, during the last two sessions some time was spent in assertion training regarding her boss and the way he had been treating her. Her 95 SUDS rating, on being told by her boss that she had an assignment to fly, alerted the therapist that in addition to her fear of flying were some interpersonal issues affecting her fear responses. She responded well to role playing and suggestions about assertively dealing with her boss.

As in systematic desensitization, practitioners of implosive therapy and flooding also postulate that a specific fear response is perpetuated by avoidance and that patients should be exposed to the feared situations until their anxiety responses extinguish. However, unlike systematic desensitization, which attempts to keep the patient in a relaxed state while presenting the anxiety-inducing stimuli, both implosion and flooding provoke an anxiety response. The patient is presented the anxiety-inducing material for relatively long periods of time—from 30 to 45 minutes—until the anxiety response begins to diminish and eventually extinguishes. The major difference between implosion and flooding is that in implosion the therapist often exaggerates and interprets the fears expressed by the patient, whereas in flooding the therapist presents the feared stimulus or situation as described by the patient until the anxiety response extinguishes.

> Mrs. Alexis's obsessive thoughts decreased from approximately 50 per day to 25 per day during the gathering of the initial baseline information. However, they still frightened her to the point that she thought she was losing her mind. After some discussion of treatment alternatives, implosion was used as a rapid method of decreasing her anxiety and diminishing the frequency of the obsessive thoughts. Several recurrent thoughts of harming her baby were developed into scenes of detailed aggression and mutilation. The patient reported a marked diminution of the obsessive thoughts after two treatment sessions (from 25 per day to 10 per day with much less anxiety). She found, however, that the implosion sessions themselves were so aversive that she decided against continuing with the technique, and the focus of therapy shifted to teaching the patient alternative methods of reducing and eliminating her negative thoughts.

Choosing an Intervention: Where to Begin

In developing a treatment program for Mrs. Alexis or Mrs. Smith, many options were available. The therapist could have used flooding and implosion with Mrs. Smith instead of systematic desensitization; e.g., presented the scenes with the highest SUDS ratings for extended periods of time, or presented exaggerated scenes based on interpretations of her fears of flying and death.

How does a therapist choose a specific treatment approach from the many exposure techniques that are available? Do the different treatment parameters and approaches affect treatment outcomes? Marks' discussion of the exposure principle might suggest that therapists could choose any technique as long as the patient is exposed to the evoking stimuli within the context of a therapeutic relationship. This theoretical hypothesis can and is being submitted to empirical study for specific anxiety disorders (2). An important component of such studies is clear specification of the therapeutic parameters that differentiate the different behavior techniques. Marks discusses these parameters in the following terms:

1. Exposure rate to the evoking stimuli (ES)—slow or fast.
2. Exposure duration to the ES—short or long, spaced (breaks between scene presentation), or massed (one presentation after another).
3. Exposure in fantasy, in vivo, or through modeling and film.
4. Exposure cues presented and controlled by therapist or by patient.
5. Exposure sessions conducted individually or in a group.

Ideally, a clinician would choose a specific treatment approach and specific treatment parameters based upon empirical data. Unfortunately, the treatment outcome literature still is unclear on the role played by various treatment parameters (2). Although it is still premature to make generalizations about treatment parameters, the following emerging trends can help clinicians make decisions about treatment:

1. In vivo treatments may be more effective than in vitro (fantasy techniques).
2. Group treatments may be more effective than individual treatments for agoraphobia and obsessive-compulsive disorders.
3. Relaxation alone does not appear to add much to treatment outcomes.

In the absence of more extensive empirical guidelines, other clinical variables still play critical roles in choosing specific treatment techniques and developing comprehensive treatment programs. Several of the obvious variables that influence treatment planning are the patient's receptivity to the techniques, the patient's assets, the patient's social and familial circumstances (who in the family should and is willing to participate in the program), and the therapist's type of practice and competence.

With Dr. Jason, the patient's assets and daily schedule were the variables that influenced the starting point of the treatment intervention. Dr. Jason's perfectionist type-A personality and his daily hospital schedule made it very difficult for him to learn to relax. Taking these variables into account the therapist began the treatment program by starting Dr. Jason on an early morning exercise program using the patient's enjoyment of exercise (he used to be a competitive runner). Cognitive-behavioral interventions of his anxiety were initiated after the patient was on a regular jogging program that was implemented without difficulty. The jogging intervention had the unexpected benefit of reducing his early morning anxiety and positively engaging him in amateur 10 kilometer competitions, which he thoroughly enjoyed.

With Mrs. Alexis, patient acceptance became the critical variable. She had a good initial response to the implosion intervention. However, after the second visit she requested a change in technique because the implosion techniques were too upsetting to her during the actual flooding sessions. She made this request even though she noticed a reduction of her disturbing thoughts after the sessions.

The clinician's day-to-day practice schedule can be a variable in limiting the range of treatment options. If the therapist cannot get away from the office for periods of time, in vivo treatments may be too difficult to implement.

Mr. Catalona's initial hospital treatment involved the therapist accompanying him on walks to the cafeteria, the gift shop, the gym, and so on. Prior to leaving the hospital, the therapist accompanied the patient in his car while he learned to drive the freeways without anxiety episodes. Eventually, the patient made his own outings unaccompanied. He was able to find an apartment and a job on his own.

Because behavioral interventions frequently involve treatment in public places and in the patient's home environment, auxiliary personnel trained in behavioral techniques can be supervised in the implementation of in vivo interventions. Marks describes the use of behaviorally trained nurses who frequently implement his exposure interventions in the patient's home environment (2).

Current Treatment Trends: Behavior Therapy with Psychopharmacology and Psychotherapy

During the past decade a major shift occurred in the paradigms that have guided psychotherapy treatment and evaluation. From the application of individual techniques or a school of psychotherapy, systematic programs were developed for specific disorders (27). The same shift is occurring within the field of behavior therapy. From the narrowly focused single interventions of the first generation of behavioral therapies, the field has matured and begun to accept the challenge of meeting the complexities of psychiatric disorders.

For example, second- and third-generation behavioral approaches have evolved into comprehensive programs such as the Mathews, Gelder, and Johnston's (28) program for agoraphobic patients and their spouses. The program is conducted at home, guided by the therapist and a client's manual. Other behavioral clinicians and researchers also recognized the need for comprehensive research and treatment strategies in treating anxiety disorders. Stampler discusses the need for such an integrated conceptual and therapeutic approach to panic disorders that includes psychodynamic, cognitive, behavioral, and interpersonal techniques as well as psychotropic medications (29).

In Chapter 6, Dr. Sheehan covered the more sophisticated understanding and use of psychotropic medications with behavioral techniques. As he noted, imipramine (30) has been shown to block the physiologic expression of panic attacks in patients with agoraphobia and phobic disorders, but patients continued to report symptoms of anticipatory anxiety and avoided social situations in which their symptoms occurred (30). With persuasion, support, and minor tranquilizers the anticipatory anxiety also was reduced. More recent work has investigated other psychotropic medications such as benzodiazepines, beta-adrenergic blockers, and monoamine oxidase inhibitors to block panic attacks (30-34). These psychotropic medications in conjunction with behavioral approaches provide the clinician with important tools to reduce patients' disabling symptoms and to improve their psychosocial functioning.

Although the combination of psychotropic medications and behavioral techniques appears to be a logical integration of approaches, some cautions still are in order. Hussain's study of brevital-assisted desensitization of phobic and agoraphobic outpatients did not demonstrate any advantage of over saline-placebo desensitization (34). Another study compared brevital-assisted flooding, standard flooding, and supportive psychotherapy in the treatment of agoraphobics. The brevital-assisted flooding demonstrated less improvement than the standard flooding, although both flooding treatments were more effective than supportive psychotherapy (35). Similar problems may exist with the benzodiazepines (31), the beta blockers (32), and tricyclic antidepressants (36).

The patient's attribution of change is an important variable that may be influencing these outcomes and accounting for the less than optimal integration of psychotropic medications with behavior therapy techniques (31). If the patient attributes the reduction in symptoms and improvement in function to the medications rather than to his or her own efforts, this may undermine any belief the patient has in effectively managing future stressful situations. The belief that "the medication caused me to improve" may also reflect an underlying belief that the patient is in some way "defective." Such beliefs should be addressed by the clinician as part of the overall treatment program. Additional steps that clinicians can implement to improve patient self-esteem and sense of self-efficacy are gradually weaning the patient from medications and exposing them to evoking stimuli while they no longer are on medications.

Besides the combination of behavior therapy and psychotropic medications, clinicians have been experimenting with combinations of behavior therapy and psychodynamic therapy described by Dr. Nemiah in Chapter 5. Rhoads and Feather reported a case study in which the desensitization hierarchy included scenes from the patient's childhood conflicts with her parents (37). Brown also presented three cases in which the behavioral treatment progressed only when important dynamic issues were integrated into a desensitization hierarchy (38). Segraves and Smith reported several cases of concurrent psychodynamic therapy and behavior therapy. Using this approach, the behavioral intervention was conducted by a consulting behavioral clinician who treated a specific symptom that was impeding the patient's progress in therapy (39). Wachtel and others also have been exploring the procedural and conceptual similarities between behavior therapy and psychodynamic therapy that may lead to a more systematic integration of techniques (40).

Conclusion

Important aspects of behavioral assessment and treatments of anxiety disorders are highlighted in this chapter. For the clinician who wants to go further, the following texts pursue in-depth both the conceptual issues and practical interventions.

Annotated Bibliography

Behavioral Assessment

Hersen M, Bellack A: Behavioral Assessment: A Practical Handbook. New York, Pergamon Press, 1976.
 As the title suggests, this book is a practical handbook of behavioral assessment. The first three chapters cover the historical background, issues of taxonomy, and the behavioral interview. The next three chapters are a particularly useful review of assessment approaches and specific evaluation instruments. Chapter 7 by Lick and Katkin specifically reviews the assessment of anxiety and fears.

Barlow DH, ed: Behavioral Assessment of Adult Disorders. New York, Guildford Press, 1981.

Nelson's chapter in this text is an excellent overview of behavioral assessment that can be used by clinicians. In addition, the chapters by Taylor and Agras and Mavissakalian and Barlow on assessment of phobias and obsessive-compulsive disorders, are both tailored to the clinician who is consulted by patients with anxiety disorders.

Behavioral Treatment of Anxiety Disorders

Marks I: Cure and Care of the Neuroses. New York, John Wiley & Sons, 1981.

Probably one of the best texts currently available for the clinician interested in the theoretical and practical aspects of anxiety disorders. Dr. Marks and his colleagues at the Maudsley have conducted some of the definitive work in this field.

Mathews AM, Gelder MG, Johnston DW: Agoraphobia: Nature and Treatment. New York, Guildford Press, 1981.

This book is an excellent overview of agoraphobia and presentation of a step-by-step, systematic treatment of agoraphobics.

Behavioral Techniques

Goldfried MR, Davison GC: Clinical Behavior Therapy. New York, Holt Rinehart Winston, 1976.

A very practical "how to do it" introduction to issues in behavioral assessment, interviewing, and establishing a therapeutic relationship. Also contains specific guides to relaxation training, systematic desensitization, behavioral rehearsal, cognitive relabeling, problem solving, and reinforcement techniques.

Rimm DC, Masters JC: Behavior Therapy: Techniques and Empirical Findings. New York, Academic Press, 1974.

A more comprehensive and detailed review of techniques than *Clinical Behavior Therapy*, this is a useful companion book to consult for more details about technique and conceptual issues.

References

1. Rimm DC, Masters JC: Behavior Therapy: Techniques and Empirical Findings. New York, Academic Press, 1974

2. Marks I: Cure and Care of Neuroses. New York, John Wiley & Sons, 1981

3. Dollard J, Miller NE: Personality and Psychotherapy: An Analysis in Terms of Learning, Thinking, and Culture. New York, McGraw-Hill, 1950

4. Wolpe J: Psychotherapy by Reciprocol Inhibition. Stanford, Stanford University Press, 1958

5. Masserman JH: Behavior and Neurosis: An Experimental Psycho-analytic Approach to Psychobiologic Principles. Chicago, University of Chicago Press, 1943

6. Seligman MEP: Helplessness. San Francisco, WH Freeman, 1975

7. Kazdin AE: History of Behavior Modification. Baltimore, University Park Press, 1978

8. Taylor CB, Liberman RL, Agras WS, et al: Treatment evaluation and behavior therapy, in Treatment Planning in Psychiatry. Edited by Lewis JM, Usdin G. Washington, DC, American Psychiatric Association, 1982

9. Skinner BF: The Behavior of Organisms: An Experimental Analysis. New York, Appleton-Century, 1938

10. Skinner BF: What is the experimental analysis of behavior? J Exp Anal Behav 9:213-218, 1966

11. Skinner BF: About Behaviorism. New York, Knopf, 1974

12. Kanfer FH, Saslow G: Behavioral diagnosis, in Behavior Therapy: Appraisal and Status. Edited by Franks CM. New York, McGraw-Hill, 1969

13. Goldfried MR, Sprafkin JN: Behavioral Personality Assessment. New Jersey, General Learning Press, 1974

14. Morganstern KP: Behavioral interviewing: the initial stages of assessment, in Behavioral Assessment. Edited by Henson M, Bellack A. Oxford, Pergamon Press, 1976

15. Cautela JR, Upper D: The behavioral inventory battery: the use of self-report measures, in Behavioral Assessment. Edited by Hersen M, Bellack A. Oxford, Pergamon Press, 1976

16. Wolpe J, Lange PJ: A fear survey schedule for use in behavior therapy. Behav Res Ther 2:27, 1964

17. Cautela JR: Behavior Analysis Forms for Clinical Intervention. Champaign, Ill., Research Press, 1983

18. Johnson SM, Bolstad O: Methodological issues in naturalistic observation: some problems and solutions for field research, in Behavior Change: Methodology, Concepts and Practice. Edited by Hammerlynck LA, Handy LC, Mash EJ. Champaign, Ill., Research Press, 1973

19. Liberman RP, DiRisi W, King L, Eckman T, Wood D: Behavioral measurement in a community mental health center, in Evaluating Behavioral Programs Community Residential and School Settings: Proceedings of the Fifth International Banff Conference on Behavior Modification. Edited by Davison P, Clark FW, Hammerlynck LA. Champaign, Ill., Research Press, 1976

20. Epstein LH: Psychophysiological measurement in assessment, in Behavioral Assessment. Edited by Herson M, Bellack A. Oxford, Pergamon Press, 1976

21. Alevizos P, DeRisi W, Liberman RP, Eckman T, Callahan E: The behavior observation instrument: a method of direct observation for program evaluation. J Appl Behav Anal 11:243-257, 1978

22. Shapiro D, Surwitt R: Biofeedback, in Behavioral Medicine: Theory and Practice. Edited by Pomerleau O, Brady JP. Baltimore, Williams & Wilkins, 1979

23. Barlow DH, Mavissakalian M, Schofield L: Patterns of desynchrony in agoraphobia. Behav Res Ther 18:441-448, 1930

24. Salter A: Conditioned Reflex Therapy. New York, Creative Age, 1949

25. Stampfl TG: Implosive therapy: a learning theory derived psychodynamic therapeutic technique, in Critical Issues in Clinical Psychology. Edited by Lebarba & Dent. New York, Academic Press, 1961

26. Jacobson E: Progressive Muscle Relaxation. Chicago, University of Chicago Press, 1929

27. Gottman J, Markman HJ: Experimental designs in psychotherapy research, in Handbook of Psychotherapy and Behavior Change, 2nd ed. Edited by Garfield SL, Bergin AE. New York, John Wiley & Sons, 1978

28. Mathews AM, Gelder MG, Johnston DW: Agoraphobia: Nature and Treatment. New York, Guilford Press, 1981

29. Stampler FM: Panic disorder: description, conceptualization, and implications for the treatment. Clin Psychol Rev 2:469-486, 1982

30. Klein DF: Delineation of two drug responsive syndromes. Psychopharmacologia 5:397-408, 1964

31. Johnston D, Gath D: Arousal levels and attribution effects in diazepam-assisted flooding. Br J Psychiatry 122:463-466, 1973

32. Hafner J, Milton F: The influence of propranolol on the exposure in vivo of agoraphobics. Psychol Med 129:378-383, 1977

33. Tyrer PJ, Candy J, Kelly DH: Phenelzine in phobic anxiety: a controlled trial. Psychol Med 3:120-124, 1973

34. Hussain MZ: Desensitization and flooding (implosion) in the treatment of phobias. Am J Psychiatry 127:1509-1514, 1971

35. Chambless DL, Foa EB, Groves GA, Goldstein AJ: Flooding with brevital in the treatment of agoraphobia: countereffective? Behav Res Ther 17:243-251, 1979

36. Zitrin CM: Combined pharmacological and psychological treatment of phobias, in Phobia: Psychological and Pharmacological Treatment. Edited by Mavissakian MR, Barlow DH. New York, Guilford Press, 1981

37. Rhoads JM, Feather BF: The application of psychodynamics to behavior therapy. Am J Psychiatry 131:17-20, 1974

38. Brown M: Psychodynamics and behavior therapy. Psychiatr Clin North America 1:435-448, 1978

39. Segraves RT, Smith RC: Concurrent psychotherapy and behavior therapy. Arch Gen Psychiatry 33:756-763, 1976

40. Wachtel PL: Psychoanalysis and Behavior Therapy. New York, Basic Books, 1977

8

Anxiety and Sleep

Robert L. Williams, M.D.
Ismet Karacan, M.D. (Med) D.Sc.

8

Anxiety and Sleep

Robert L. Williams, M.D.
Ismet Karacan, M.D. (Med) D.Sc.

The association between anxiety and sleep is not a new idea. The fact that anxious patients have trouble falling asleep and maintaining uninterrupted sleep has been widely studied and reported. Patients themselves recognize the connection between feeling nervous and upset and not being able to sleep. A patient who does manage to fall asleep often complains of awakening several times during the night. The result is a patient who adds inability to sleep to a list of worries.

Two of the major contributors to disturbed sleep are autonomic arousal and intrusive cognition. These symptoms of anxiety are also components of the clinically accepted definition of anxiety. The *Diagnostic Classification of Sleep and Arousal Disorders*, published in 1979 by the Association of Sleep Disorders Centers (ASDC), notes that autonomic arousal and intrusive cognition are involved in two categories of disorders of initiating and maintaining sleep (DIMS), formerly called insomnia. The two categories are the persistent psychophysiological type and DIMS associated with psychiatric disorders, mainly symptom and personality.

These categories are prevalent diagnoses in sleep disorders centers as reported by Coleman and his colleagues in 1982 (1). A national cooperative study was undertaken between 1978 and 1980 by 11 sleep disorders centers. Using the above-mentioned classification system and polysomnography as a basis for diagnosing sleep-wake disorders, a total of 3,900 patients with sleep-wake complaints were examined. Nearly one-third presented with insomnia. Thirty-five percent of DIMS patients studied fell into the category of psychiatric disorders, which was the most prevalent diagnosis for these patients and the third most prevalent among all patients with sleep-wake problems. Psychophysiological insomnia involving somatized tension and anxiety accounted for 15 percent of DIMS patients and was the second most prevalent diagnosis (Table 8-1). Personality disorders involving anxiety accounted for 45 percent of the psychiatric disorders (Table 8-2). These studies indicate that almost one-half of all insomnia conditions involve symptoms of anxiety. These findings were supported by a Stanford Sleep Disorders Center study of 129 sequential insomniacs from 1975 to 1978. The investigators found that 36 percent exhibited persistent psychophysiological DIMS and 12 percent showed personality disorders and major psychoses (2).

Table 8-1. Prevalent Diagnoses of Insomnia

Psychiatric Disorders	35%
Psychophysiological	15%
Drug/alcohol dependency	12%
Myoclonus/restless legs	12%

Note: Patients presenting with complaints of insomnia (DIMS) in a multicenter survey were found to have one or more of the diagnoses listed above. The remaining 26 percent included patients with no significant pathological finding (9 percent), sleep apnea syndrome (6 percent), and medical-toxic and childhood-onset insomnia (11 percent).

Source: Coleman et al., 1982. Reprinted with permission.

Table 8-2. Prevalence of Insomnia Diagnoses Associated with
Psychiatric Disorders

Major affective disorder	50%
Personality disorder	45%
Psychosis	5%

Note: Patients presenting with complaints of insomnia (DIMS) who were
found to have a psychiatric disorder could be further classified into
one of the above categories.

Source: Coleman et al., 1982. Reprinted with permission.

Persistent Psychophysiological DIMS

Persistent psychophysiological DIMS is classified as sleep
onset and intermediary sleep maintenance insomnia. This
condition develops as a result of the mutually reinforcing
factors of chronic, somatized tension-anxiety and negative
conditioning to sleep. It may also evolve from situational
insomnia when a recent, distressing event has occurred
and the reaction persists beyond three weeks after the
event's resolution.

In this category of DIMS, resting muscle activity remains
high in sleep, with rapid pulse rate and alpha-like activity
also recorded. The patient is troubled by repetitive awakenings associated with worrisome thoughts and anxious
dreams. Anxiety is generally not sensed as such but rather
somatized as restlessness, motor tension, autonomic hyperactivity, apprehensive expectation, ruminative
thoughts, hypervigilance, excessive visual scanning, and
the like. Apprehension about falling asleep builds from the
patient's trying too hard to do so, and this in turn causes
arousal of the central nervous system, which becomes a
conditioned internal factor. Conditioning elements are thus
self-perpetuating.

Patients reported being able to sleep better during
nonwork periods such as weekends and vacations when
the stress of school or work was lowered. These patients
tended to consider themselves as light sleepers and it
seemed that psychosocial and vocational stresses tended to
exacerbate psychophysiological DIMS.

DIMS Associated with Psychiatric Disorders

Like persistent psychophysiological DIMS, insomnia associated with psychiatric disorders creates problems in sleep onset and intermediary sleep maintenance. DIMS associated with symptom and personality disorders are clearly related to psychological and behavioral symptoms of clinically classified (DSM-III) nonaffective and nonpsychotic psychiatric disorders.

Precipitating conditions exhibited by patients include generalized anxiety, panic and phobic disorders, hypochondriasis, obsessive-compulsive disorder, personality disorder, and similar disorders formerly known as neurotic syndromes. Many of these disorders represent unsuccessful attempts to control anxiety either by personality or behavioral modifications. They also represent maladaptation to inward and outward needs or to stress, or the anxiety itself may result from a longstanding conscious or unconscious psychological conflict. Overt and uncontrolled anxiety, then, seems to be responsible for difficulty in falling asleep in these patients.

Because of the similarities between them, persistent psychophysiologic DIMS and DIMS associated with personality and symptom disorders may be difficult to distinguish at diagnosis. The insomniac with compulsive symptoms, for example, may also have considerable somatized anxiety.

Clinical Studies

To further complicate the diagnostic process, insomnia caused by anxiety and insomnia caused by depression often accompany one another and present similar polysomnographic findings (3). In addition, depressed patients have high levels of psychophysiological arousal. However, short latency to rapid eye movement (REM) sleep, considered a biological marker of depression, can help distinguish major affective disorder from anxiety as the major cause of sleep disturbance. The importance and the difficulty in distinguishing insomnia secondary to anxiety from insomnia secondary to depression is illustrated by the following case report.

Mr. HR is a 40-year-old, white, married commodities broker, who was referred to the Baylor Sleep Disorders Center for evaluation of his complaints of insomnia. The patient was very successful in his business and was one of the most productive brokers in his company, but he described some problems at work that centered around disagreements with his secretary. Initially, he reported that he was happily married.

Because of increasing difficulty sleeping, Mr. HR consulted the referring physician. Although he usually was able to get to sleep, he would awaken every night around 3:00 A.M. and have difficulty getting back to sleep. When he awakened he was, by his description, hyperalert. The patient complained that he often dreamed of the commodities market tape, and when he awakened he frequently rehashed the fluctuations of the market in his mind. He had been given various hypnotics, each of which worked for a few days, but typically after ten days to two weeks they seemed to lose their effectiveness.

The clinical evaluation suggested that Mr. HR was an aggressive, typical type A personality, and the preliminary impression was that he was experiencing increasing anxiety that stemmed from his conflicts at work and his excessive preoccupation with the market, all of which disrupted his sleep. (Actually, he slept quite well in the sleep laboratory.) However, a battery of psychological screening tests suggested a mood disorder rather than an anxiety state. This was explored with the patient in a series of interviews, and within a couple of weeks it became apparent that he was so depressed that it was necessary to admit him to the hospital for treatment. As more information was produced the patient revealed that all was not well with his marriage and his problems had been compounded by his involvement in an extramarital affair. Treatment of his depression with medication relieved his symptoms and markedly improved his sleep.

It is not unusual for patients to present initially to their physician or to a sleep disorders center complaining of insomnia before they are aware of, or admit to, depression. The sleep complaint is sometimes seen as a ticket for admission, so to speak, which is easier for some patients to admit to than emotional problems.

Earlier clinical studies support the existence of the connection between sleep-wake problems and anxiety. In

1950, Cohen and White reported a relationship between insomnia and anxious-neurotic patients. Whereas only 4 percent of normal controls were unable to sleep, 54 percent of anxious subjects exhibited insomnia (4). Other researchers observed the same personality traits described in Mr. HR (5) as well as the concern of the patient about his inability to fall asleep (6-9). A study of 376 psychiatric patients by Stonehill and his colleagues reaffirmed the hypothesis of anxious patients having longer sleep latency (10).

Drug Studies

The relationship between anxiety and sleep also is indicated in drug studies. Researchers studied several benzodiazepines, known for their hypnotic and anxiolytic properties, and which, according to the patients themselves, demonstrated improved sleep quality and reduced anxiety scores. Zimmerman, Tansella, and Lader designed their study to assess the clinical effects of diazepam and amylobarbitone and the psychological performance of the patient one week after treatment. Diazepam improved subjective anxiety and insomnia in patients with anxiety neurosis, but amylobarbitone improved only the quality of sleep (11). Hindmarch and Parrott found that giving dipotassium chlorazepate and clobazam at bedtime not only improved the quality of sleep but also reduced scores the next day (12). Other studies also show that giving chlormezanone (Trancopal) at bedtime improves sleep quality and relieves mild neurotic anxiety (13,14).

Sleep Laboratory Studies

To supplement information gathered during psychological testing and interviews, electroencephalographic (EEG) recordings of sleep can be most important. Results of sleep lab studies attempting to link anxiety with sleep-wake problems, however, vary. This can be attributed to differences among sleep lab facilities, patient population, approach of the study, or experience of the researchers.

Sleep lab research, therefore, does not offer a firm confirmation of the adverse effect of anxiety on sleep. Although the indications are there, sleep lab researchers can only count anxiety among several possible causes of disturbed sleep. Anxiety in the insomniac may be secondary to depression, the major cause of disturbed sleep. Sleep is studied in two ways in the lab: either anxiety is induced in normal subjects, or the anxiety scales of insomnia patients who have been evaluated by EEG are reviewed. There are questions as to whether or not anxiety-induced normals represent valid subjects. Also in question are the effects of other possible psychiatric disturbances on insomnia patients, especially if they are not mentioned in the study.

It is generally accepted that when anxiety is induced in normal subjects, sleep latency and arousals increase, but REM sleep seems to be unaffected. Using psychological testing, Goodenough and others documented the anxiety of normal subjects by showing them a disturbing documentary film just before they went to bed (15). Although the subjects exhibited sleep-onset insomnia, researchers could not be certain it was caused by anxiety and not by depression or hostility, which according to the tests, were also present. Both Lester and others and McDonald and others studied medical and university students' reactions to examinations and found a correlation between anxiety and increased galvanic skin response and reduced slow-wave sleep (16,17).

Although results vary, they seem to tentatively support the hypothesis that arousal associated with anxiety does disturb sleep in anxiety-induced normal subjects. Monroe suggested that the physiologic result of anxiety might be responsible for increased arousal in DIMS patients (18). Likewise, Kazarian and others reported support for both arousal and stimulus control models of insomnia (19). Results of the Manifest Anxiety Test given to inpatients at a psychiatric hospital distinguished between patients reporting sleep-wake problems and those reporting none. Foster and others further support the idea in a limited study of ten anxious patients (3). These patients showed a significant increase in sleep latency but decreases in total sleep time, efficiency of sleep, and delta sleep. They also found, however, that the results were similar to those of depressed patients. In 1979, Ware reported that patients presenting to the Baylor Sleep Disorders Center complaining of disturbed sleep had high anxiety scores on test scales (20).

On the negative side, Freedman and Papsdorf failed to find a relationship between presleep autonomic activity and sleep-onset insomnia (21). At the Peter Bent Brigham Sleep Clinic, Regestein found no causal relationship between anxiety and insomnia (22).

In an attempt to clarify these inconsistencies, we planned a controlled study with our colleagues at the Baylor College of Medicine Sleep Disorders Center in 1979. Twenty-five control-matched DIMS patients were divided into two groups and either given mood-or sleep-altering drugs or no drugs at all. The subjects' anxiety was measured using several indices, including the Profile of Mood States t-scale (POMS-T), the State-Trait Anxiety Index, and some indices derived from the Minnesota Multiphasic Personality Inventory (MMPI). The usual sleep EEG recordings were also made on each subject. With the exception of a positive correlation between sleep latency and anxiety in the drug group, we found the subjects' disturbed sleep was not caused by anxiety. The DIMS patients in the nondrug group exhibited more anxiousness and depression than the controls. They also experienced increased latency and decreased efficiency of sleep. Covariance analyses showed that age differences and depression between the subject groups accounted for the altered sleep patterns, and that increased anxiety is related to sleep latency when covaried with depression. The patients in the drug group showed more extreme changes on psychological measurements. These results may reflect the fact that subjects were selected because of sleep-wake problems and not necessarily because of anxiety symptoms (Figures 8-1 to 8-3) (23).

Hypothesis

The studies presented lead us to hypothesize that the factor causing insomnia is related to the degree that the patient

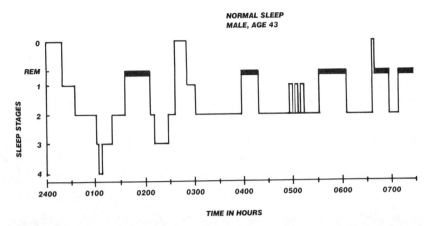

Figure 8-1. Histogram of all-night sleep recording of normal male. Note the short sleep latency and the minimal amount of wakefulness during the night. Characteristic of normal sleep, too, is the early night progression through the non-REM stages into deep sleep. Typically, following this, is the initial REM period, about 90 minutes after sleep onset. The four REM periods (the last hour of the night is, essentially, one REM period) accounts for 23 percent of the total sleep time, both normal parameters.

Source: Williams et al., 1979. Reprinted with permission.

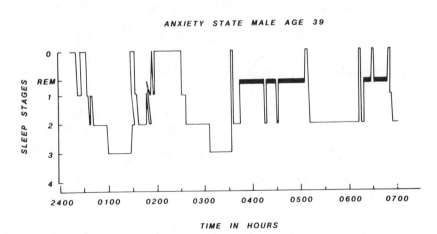

Figure 8-2. Histogram of the all-night sleep of a patient complaining of insomnia and suffering from an anxiety state. As compared to the normal, note the longer sleep latency and the numerous and lengthy awakenings. Additionally, there is a failure to achieve Stage 4 deep sleep, and a very delayed initial REM period.

Source: Williams et al., 1979. Reprinted with permission.

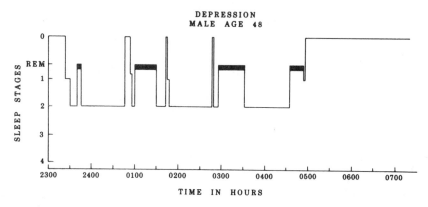

Figure 8-3. Histogram of the all-night sleep of a patient complaining of insomnia and suffering from depression. Again, as compared to the normal histogram, note the absence of deep sleep (Stages 3 and 4) altogether. Also note the frequent awakenings, especially the early morning arousal. REM sleep appears earlier in the night than in a normal, and the REM sleep itself is characterized by a REM density (i.e., frequency of eye movements) that is strikingly different from a normal REM period.

Source: Williams et al., 1979. Reprinted with permission.

internalizes psychologically stressful situations. We think that poor sleepers seem to internalize conflicts more often, resulting in increased emotional and physical activity during sleep. This idea is consistent with the characteristics of insomniac patients classified by the ASDC as persistent psychophysiological DIMS.

Healey and others also supported this hypothesis in a retrospective study of 31 good and 31 poor sleep subjects. The researchers discovered that insomniacs were subjected to significantly more stressful life events during the year insomnia began compared with previous or subsequent years and compared to normal, good sleepers. Why, then, are such episodes of sleeplessness transient for most people while becoming chronic for others? The poor sleepers seemed more vulnerable to stress because of possible biologic and genetic makeup as well as the environmental factors of conditioning and learning. They recalled more illness, problems at home, unhappy childhood, and other anxiety-producing events (5).

Insomnia may be a maladaptive coping mechanism to

stress. Healey's poor sleep subjects reported feeling tense, nervous, or depressed. As a group they were troubled and unhappy, and faced life with apprehension to discharge strong emotion or to cope with stress on an overt behavioral level.

Thoresen and associates noted the same characteristics in their subjects. In this self-reported study of the sleep characteristics associated with anxiety, patients were assessed by means of all-night home polysomnography, sleep diaries, and psychosocial questionnaires. There were 10 normal subjects and 34 sleep-disturbed subjects. Those with sleep disturbances were categorized as follows: sleep latency, 9; sleep maintenance problems, 11; and combined problems, 14. The disturbed sleepers reported impatient and anxious behaviors; upset with routine events and chronic, daily stress; and noticeable tension and depression. These characteristics were reported at significantly higher levels in those patients with sleep onset and maintenance problems (24).

So, this state of increased physiologic activity and emotional upset in the DIMS patient perpetuates sleep-wake problems. Obviously, sleep and arousal cannot coexist. Two studies exploring the relationship between physiologic arousal and DIMS have been reported. Monroe studied the greater degree of central nervous system activity in poor sleepers (18), and his work was confirmed by Johns and others, who measured the adrenocortical steroid levels in similar subjects (25).

Treatment

Insomnia (DIMS) related to any of the conditions described earlier usually is relieved when the basic disorder is treated. However, there are a number of patients whose insomnia is not clearly related to one of the described conditions or does not improve with the correction of the basic disorder. There are also patients who have so-called essential insomnia, meaning that they do not have, or clinicians were unable to find, any condition other than a persistent insomnia. In either group the first task is to convince patients that insomnia itself is never fatal and, further, if they will refrain from taking medications that depress brain activity they will eventually get the sleep needed. In addition to convincing patients of that basic premise, it is important to encourage them to practice good sleep hygiene. This can be particularly important in the elderly insomniac. Observing a few simple rules can often relieve or markedly alleviate the problem.

1. The patient should not go to bed unless he is sleepy.
2. If awakened and unable to fall asleep again readily, the patient should get up and do something such as read or engage in some activity that is not particularly stimulating. This might or might not include watching television, depending on the program. It is important for the patient not to lie in bed struggling to get to sleep.
3. Caffeine and alcohol should be avoided in the evening. Although alcohol may shorten sleep latency, i.e., the time needed to get to sleep, it almost invariably causes the patient to awaken about three or four hours later.
4. For some patients a light snack and some warm milk helps bring about sleep onset.
5. It is important to have a regular arousal time in the morning, whatever a night's sleep has been. Such a structuring of the day usually leads to a more regular sleep onset time.

Relaxation Therapy

There are, of course, some patients for whom these measures do not work, or who are unable to follow them, and it may be necessary to try other measures. Relaxation therapy seems to help some DIMS patients. Coursey and others tested electromyographic biofeedback and autogenic training in 22 sleep-onset insomniacs. One-half of the subjects showed improvement over the one-month followup period (26). Hauri and colleagues replicated previous findings in their study of 16 subjects, 8 tense and 8 relaxed. The tense insomniacs with psychophysiological DIMS improved with relaxation therapy, and those without excess tension responded better to biofeedback training (27). Duguay and others also found relaxation training helpful to DIMS patients with high scores on depression, anxiety, and hypochondriasis scales. In their study, 6 subjects received training and 6 did not. Those receiving training showed improvement on all scales after five weeks of therapy (28).

Drug Therapy

Some patients respond well to l-tryptophan. We usually recommend starting with 1,000 mg at bedtime and increasing to 2,000 mg if necessary. Certain researchers have recommended higher doses, but in our experience if the patient does not respond to 1,500 or 2,000 mg, he or she usually does not do any better on the higher doses. L-tryptophan is, of course, a natural amino-acid with no side effects or complications.

We are often asked about the use of hypnotics when definitive workup has revealed no obvious etiology, and the patient has not responded to the practice of good sleep hygiene or any of the other measures just described.

There are patients, obviously, for whom a sleeping medication is indicated. Unfortunately, there is no ideal hypnotic. Whatever is prescribed should be used for only a few days or intermittently. Definitive studies on both hypnotics and benzodiazepines show the effects of both are well established. Sleep architecture is disrupted to varying degrees by all the sedative/hypnotics and benzodiazepines (REM density and period suppression, decreased delta sleep, increased beta activity, and so on). These effects contribute to the familiar cycle of increasing dosage, adding medications, habituation, and addiction. The National Academy of Sciences' report, "Sleeping Pills, Insomnia and Medical Practice," reviewed the problem of the safety and usefulness of hypnotic drugs and examined physicians' prescribing practices (29). The study describes how some prescribing practices may lead to the spiral of tolerance, increased dosage, additional drugs, and usually poorer sleep.

For the occasional hypnotic, 1,500 mg of chloral hydrate at bedtime can be useful. Some patients tolerate 1,500 mg of triclofos sodium better because they do not experience the gastric distress that some patients complain of with chloral hydrate. The short-acting benzodiazepines, such as temazepam, have also been useful for the occasional hypnotic prescription. The benzodiazepines with a longer half-life, such as flurazepam (60-120 hours) are effective and usually do not cause problems on single administration. If they are given several nights in a row, however, they often lead to difficulties as a result of the accumulation of higher and higher blood levels.

For years, physicians have described patients who routinely take one or two aspirin tablets at bedtime and claim that this has helped their sleep. Until recently it was speculated that if there were any medicinal effects, they might be due to the relief of some accumulated aches and pains. However, a more recent study suggests that the aspirin may actually increase the brain serotonin levels, which may, in turn, enhance sleep (30).

Summary

Although objective and subjective information about anxiety and sleep-wake problems seems to indicate that there is a relationship between anxiety and disturbed sleep, the variability of anxiety's effects on sleep, measured in DIMS patients and anxiety-induced normal patients, seems to point toward only a secondary connection. Test results indicate that to establish an unequivocal, primary link between anxiety and DIMS, researchers must be able to separate anxiety from the other psychiatric disturbances it usually accompanies. Anxiety and depression are often concomitant, and we are unsure whether anxiety-associated sleep disturbances are primary or secondary to depression.

With the help of advanced computer technology, sleep lab researchers may further contribute to resolving this question by providing more sensitive EEG measurements that detect the differences between anxious and normal subjects. Additional drug studies researching the actions of benzodiazepines as they relate to anxiety and disturbed sleep may also shed more light on the question and perhaps contribute to its resolution.

References

1. Coleman RM, Roffwarg HP, Kennedy SJ, et al: Sleep-wake disorders based on a polysomnographic diagnosis. A national cooperative study. JAMA 247(7):997-1003, 1982

2. Sherer M, Zarcone V, Kraemer, H, Dement WC, van den Hoed J, Mitler MM: Insomnia: clinical and polysomnographic findings in patients presenting with the complaint of difficulty in initiating and maintaining sleep. APSS 1981 (Abstract)

3. Foster G, Grau T, Spiker DG, et al: EEG sleep in generalized anxiety disorder. Sleep Research 6:145, 1977 (Abstract)

4. Cohen M, White P: Life situations, emotions and neurocirculatory asthenia (anxiety neurosis, neurasthenia effort syndrome). Res Publ Assoc Res Nerv Ment Dis 29:832-869, 1950

5. Healey ES, Kales A, Monroe LK, et al: Onset insomnia: role of life-stress events. Psychosom Med 43(5):439-451, 1981

6. Coursey RD, Frankel BL, Gaarder KR, Mott DE: A comparison of relaxation techniques with electrosleep therapy for chronic, sleep-onset insomnia; a sleep-EEG study. Biofeedback and Self Regulation 5:57-73, 1980

7. Kales A, Caldwell AB, Preston TA, Healey S, Kales JD: Personality patterns in insomnia. Arch Gen Psychiatry 33:1128-1134, 1976

8. Ascher LM, Efran JS: Use of paradoxical intention in a behavioral program for sleep onset insomnia. J Consult Clin Psychol 46:547-550, 1978

9. Storms MD, Nisbett RE: Insomnia and the attribution process. J Pers Soc Psychol 16:319-328, 1970

10. Stonehill E, Crisp AH, Koval J: The relationship of reported sleep characteristics to psychiatric diagnosis and mood. Br J Med Psychol 49:381, 1976

11. Zimmerman C, Tansella M, Lader M: A comparison of the clinical and psychological effects of diazepam and amylobarbitone in anxious patients. J Clin Pharmacol 7:605-611, 1979

12. Hindmarch I, Parrott AC: The effects of repeated nocturnal doses of clobazam, dipotassium chlorazepate and placebo on subjective ratings of sleep and early morning behavior and objective measures of arousal, psychomotor performance and anxiety. J Clin Pharmacol 8:325-329, 1979

13. Ali-Khan G: Treatment of anxiety-related insomnia with chlormezanone. Curr Med Res Opin 6:259-262, 1979

14. Warnock JMT: A controlled study of trancopal in the treatment of sleep disturbances due to anxiety. J Int Med Res 6:115-120, 1978

15. Goodenough DR, Witkin HA, Koulack O, Cohen H: The effects of stress films on dream affect and on respiration and eye-movement activity during rapid-eye-movement sleep. Psychophysiology 12:313-320, 1975

16. Lester BK, Burch NR, Dossett RC: Nocturnal EEG-GSR profiles: The influence on presleep states. Psychophysiology 3:238-248, 1967

17. McDonald DG, Shallenberger HD, Koresko RL, Kenzy BG: Studies of spontaneous electrodermal responses in sleep. Psychophysiology 13:128-134, 1976

18. Monroe LJ: Psychological and physiological differences between good and poor sleepers. J Abnormal Psychol 72:255, 1967

19. Karzarian SS, Howe MG, Merskey H, Deinum EJL: Insomnia: anxiety, sleep-incompatible behaviors and depression. J Clin Psychol 34:865-869, 1978

20. Ware JC: The symptom of insomnia: causes and cures. Psychiatric Annals 9:27-49, 1979

21. Freedman R, Papsdorf JD: Biofeedback and progressive relaxation treatment of sleep onset insomnia: a controlled all night investigation. Biofeedback Self-Control 1:253-271, 1976

22. Regestein OR: Practical ways to manage chronic insomnia. Med Times 107:19-23, 1979

23. Williams RL, Ware JC, Ilaria RL, Karacan I: Disturbed sleep and anxiety, in Phenomenology and Treatment of Anxiety. Edited by Fann WE, Karacan I, Pokorny AD, Williams, RL. New York, Spectrum, 1979

24. Thoresen CE, Burnett KF, Rosekind MR, Bracke P, Kirmil-Gray K, Dexter G, Clark J: Psychosocial contrasts between normal and sleep disturbed subjects with onset, maintenance and combined complaints. APSS 10:236, 1981

25. Johns MW, Gay TJA, Masterson JP, Bruce DW: Relationship between sleep habits, adrenocortical activity and personality. Psychosom Med 33:499-508, 1981

26. Coursey RD, Buchsbaum M, Frankel BL: Personality measures and evoked responses in chronic insomniacs. J Abnorm Psychol 84:239-249, 1975

27. Hauri P, Percy L, Hartmann E, Russ D: Treating psychophysiological insomnia with biofeedback, a replication. APSS 10:167, 1981 (Abstract)

28. Duguay M, Gagnon I, Montplaisir J: The treatment of idiopathic insomnia by relaxation therapy. APSS 10:192, 1981 (Abstract)

29. Sleeping Pills, Insomnia, and Medical Practice, Washington, Institute of Medicine, National Academy of Sciences, 1979

30. Hauri P, Silberfarb PM: The effects of aspirin on the sleep of insomniacs. Sleep Res 7:100, 1978

Appendix

The material in this Appendix has been excerpted from the *Diagnostic and Statistical Manual of Mental Disorders*, Third Edition (DSM-III), published in 1980 by the American Psychiatric Association, 1400 K Street, N.W., Washington, DC 20005.

Anxiety Disorders

In this group of disorders anxiety is either the predominant disturbance, as in Panic Disorder and Generalized Anxiety Disorder, or anxiety is experienced if the individual attempts to master the symptoms, as in confronting the dreaded object or situation in a Phobic Disorder or resisting the obsessions or compulsions in Obsessive Compulsive Disorder. Diagnosis of an Anxiety Disorder is not made if the anxiety is due to another disorder, such as Schizophrenia, an Affective Disorder, or an Organic Mental Disorder.

It has been estimated that from 2% to 4% of the general population has at some time had a disorder that this manual would classify as an Anxiety Disorder.

Panic Disorder, Phobic Disorders and Obsessive Compulsive Disorder are each apparently more common among family members of individuals with each of these disorders than in the general population.

PHOBIC DISORDERS (OR PHOBIC NEUROSES)

The essential feature is persistent and irrational fear of a specific object, activity, or situation that results in a compelling desire to avoid the dreaded object, activity, or situation (the phobic stimulus). The fear is recognized by the individual as excessive or unreasonable in proportion to the actual dangerousness of the object, activity, or situation.

Irrational avoidance of objects, activities, or situations that has an insignificant effect on life adjustment is commonplace. For example, many individuals experience some irrational fear when unable to avoid contact with harmless insects or spiders, but this has no major effect on their lives. However, when the avoidance behavior or fear is a significant source of distress to the individual or interferes with social or role functioning, a diagnosis of a Phobic Disorder is warranted.

The Phobic Disorders are subdivided into three types: Agoraphobia, the most severe and pervasive form; Social Phobia; and Simple Phobia. Both Social and Simple Phobias generally involve a circumscribed stimulus, but Simple Phobia tends to have an earlier onset and better prognosis. When more than one type is present, multiple diagnoses should be made.

Although anxiety related to separation from parental figures is a form of phobic reaction, it is classified as Separation Anxiety Disorder, in the section Disorders Usually First Evident in Infancy, Childhood, or Adolescence (p. 50). Similarly, phobic avoidance limited to sexual activities is classified as a Psychosexual Disorder Not Elsewhere Classified (p. 282).

Although Simple Phobia is the most common type of Phobic Disorder in the general population, Agoraphobia is the most common among those seeking treatment.

300.21   Agoraphobia with Panic Attacks

300.22   Agoraphobia without Panic Attacks

The essential feature is a marked fear of being alone, or being in public places from which escape might be difficult or help not available in case of sudden incapacitation. Normal activities are increasingly constricted as the fears or avoidance behavior dominate the individual's life. The most common situations avoided involve being in crowds, such as on a busy street or in crowded stores, or being in tunnels, on bridges, on elevators, or on public transportation. Often these individuals insist that a family member or friend accompany them whenever they leave home.

The disturbance is not due to a major depressive episode, Obsessive Compulsive Disorder, Paranoid Personality Disorder, or Schizophrenia.

Often the initial phase of the disorder consists of recurrent panic attacks. (For a description of panic attacks, see p. 230.) The individual develops anticipatory fear of having such an attack and becomes reluctant or refuses to enter a variety of situations that are associated with these attacks. When there is a history of panic attacks (which may or may not be currently present) associated with avoidance behavior, the diagnosis of Agoraphobia with Panic Attacks should be made. Where there is no such history (or this information is lacking), the diagnosis of Agoraphobia without Panic Attacks should be made.

Associated features. Depression, anxiety, rituals, minor "checking" compulsions, or rumination is frequently present.

Age at onset. Most frequently the onset is in the late teens or early 20s, but it can be much later.

Course. The severity of the disturbance waxes and wanes, and periods of complete remission are possible. The activities or situations that the individual dreads may change from day to day.

Impairment. During exacerbations of the illness the individual may be housebound. The avoidance of certain situations, such as being in elevators, may grossly interfere with social and occupational functioning.

Complications. Some individuals attempt to relieve their anxiety with alcohol, barbiturates, or antianxiety medications even to the extent of becoming physiologically dependent on them. Major Depression is another complication.

Predisposing factors. Separation Anxiety Disorder in childhood and sudden object loss apparently predispose to the development of Agoraphobia.

Prevalence. A study of the general population in a small city found that approximately 0.5% of the population had had Agoraphobia at some time.

Sex ratio. The disorder is more frequently diagnosed in women.

Differential diagnosis. In **Schizophrenia, Major Depression, Obsessive Compulsive Disorder** and **Paranoid Personality Disorder** there may be phobic avoidance of certain situations. The diagnosis of Agoraphobia is not made if a phobia is due to any of these disorders.

Diagnostic criteria for Agoraphobia

A. The individual has marked fear of and thus avoids being alone or in public places from which escape might be difficult or help not available in case of sudden incapacitation, e.g., crowds, tunnels, bridges, public transportation.

B. There is increasing constriction of normal activities until the fears or avoidance behavior dominate the individual's life.

C. Not due to a major depressive episode, Obsessive Compulsive Disorder, Paranoid Personality Disorder, or Schizophrenia.

300.23   Social Phobia

The essential feature is a persistent, irrational fear of, and compelling desire to avoid, situations in which the individual may be exposed to scrutiny by others. There is also fear that the individual may behave in a manner that will be humiliating or embarrassing. Marked anticipatory anxiety occurs if the individual is confronted with the necessity of entering into such a situation, and he or she therefore attempts to avoid it. The disturbance is a significant source of distress and is recognized by the individual as excessive or unreasonable. It is not due to any other mental disorder. Examples of Social Phobias are fears of speaking or performing in public, using public lavatories, eating in public, and writing in the presence of others. Generally an individual has only one Social Phobia.

Usually the individual is aware that the fear is that others will detect signs of anxiety in the phobic situation. For example, the individual with a fear of writing in the presence of others is concerned that others may detect a hand tremor. A vicious cycle may be created in which the irrational fear generates anxiety that impairs performance, thus providing an apparent justification for avoiding the phobic situation.

Associated features. Considerable unfocused or generalized anxiety may also be present. Agoraphobia or Simple Phobia may coexist with Social Phobia.

Age at onset. The disorder often begins in late childhood or early adolescence.

Course. The disorder is usually chronic, and may undergo exacerbation when the anxiety impairs performance of the feared activity. This then leads to increased anxiety, which strengthens the phobic avoidance.

Impairment. Unless the disorder is severe, it is rarely, in itself, incapacitating. However, considerable inconvenience may result from the need to avoid the phobic situation, e.g., avoiding a trip if it would necessitate the use of a public lavatory. Fear of public speaking may interfere with professional advancement.

Complications. Individuals with this disorder are prone to the episodic abuse of alcohol, barbiturates, and antianxiety medications, which they may use to relieve their anxiety.

Prevalence. The disorder is apparently relatively rare.

Predisposing factors, sex ratio, and familial pattern. No information.

Differential diagnosis. Avoidance of certain social situations that are normally a source of some distress, which is common in many individuals with "normal" fear of public speaking, does not justify a diagnosis of Social Phobia. In **Schizophrenia, Major Depression, Obsessive Compulsive Disorder,** and **Paranoid** and **Avoidant Personality Disorders,** there may be marked anxiety and avoidance of certain social situations. However, the diagnosis of Social Phobia is not made if the phobia is due to any of these disorders.

In **Simple Phobia** there is also a circumscribed phobic stimulus, but it is not a social situation involving the possibility of humiliation or embarrassment.

Diagnostic criteria for Social Phobia

A. A persistent, irrational fear of, and compelling desire to avoid, a situation in which the individual is exposed to possible scrutiny by others and fears that he or she may act in a way that will be humiliating or embarrassing.

B. Significant distress because of the disturbance and recognition by the individual that his or her fear is excessive or unreasonable.

C. Not due to another mental disorder, such as Major Depression or Avoidant Personality Disorder.

300.29 Simple Phobia

The essential feature is a persistent, irrational fear of, and compelling desire to avoid, an object or a situation other than being alone or in public places away from home (Agoraphobia), or of humiliation or embarrassment in certain social situations (Social Phobia). Thus, this is a residual category of Phobic Disorder. This disturbance is a significant source of distress, and the individual recognizes that his or her fear is excessive or unreasonable. The disturbance is not due to another mental disorder.

Simple Phobias are sometimes referred to as "specific" phobias. The most common Simple Phobias in the general population, though not necessarily among those seeking treatment, involve animals, particularly dogs, snakes, insects, and mice. Other Simple Phobias are claustrophobia (fear of closed spaces) and acrophobia (fear of heights).

Associated features. When suddenly exposed to the phobic stimulus, the individual becomes overwhelmingly fearful and may experience symptoms identical with those of a panic attack (p. 230). Because of anticipatory anxiety, the individual will often try to gain considerable information before entering situations in which the phobic stimulus may be encountered.

Age at onset. Age at onset varies, but animal phobias nearly always begin in childhood.

Course. Most simple phobias that start in childhood disappear without treatment. However, those that persist into adulthood rarely remit without treatment.

Impairment. Impairment may be minimal if the phobic object is rare and easily avoided, such as fear of snakes in someone living in the city. Impairment may be considerable if the phobic object is common and cannot be avoided, such as a fear of elevators in someone living in a large city who must use elevators at work.

Complications and predisposing factors. No information.

Prevalence. Simple Phobias may be common; but since they rarely result in marked impairment, individuals with Simple Phobia rarely seek treatment.

Sex ratio. The disorder is more often diagnosed in women.

Differential diagnosis. In **Schizophrenia** certain activities may be avoided in response to delusions. Similarly, in **Obsessive Compulsive Disorder** phobic avoidance of certain situations that are associated with anxiety about dirt or contamination is frequent. The diagnosis of Simple Phobia should not be made in either case.

Diagnostic criteria for Simple Phobia

A. A persistent, irrational fear of, and compelling desire to avoid, an object or a situation other than being alone, or in public places away from home (Agoraphobia), or of humiliation or embarrassment in certain social situations (Social Phobia). Phobic objects are often animals, and phobic situations frequently involve heights or closed spaces.

B. Significant distress from the disturbance and recognition by the individual that his or her fear is excessive or unreasonable.

C. Not due to another mental disorder, such as Schizophrenia or Obsessive Compulsive Disorder.

ANXIETY STATES (OR ANXIETY NEUROSES)

300.01 Panic Disorder

The essential features are recurrent panic (anxiety) attacks that occur at times unpredictably, though certain situations, e.g., driving a car, may become associated with a panic attack. The same clinical picture occurring during marked physical exertion or a life-threatening situation is not termed a panic attack.

The panic attacks are manifested by the sudden onset of intense apprehension, fear, or terror, often associated with feelings of impending doom. The most common symptoms experienced during an attack are dyspnea; palpitations; chest pain or discomfort; choking or smothering sensations; dizziness, vertigo, or unsteady feelings; feelings of unreality (depersonalization or derealization); paresthesias; hot and cold flashes; sweating; faintness; trembling or shaking; and fear of dying, going crazy, or doing something uncontrolled during the attack. Attacks usually last minutes; more rarely, hours.

A common complication of this disorder is the development of an anticipatory fear of helplessness or loss of control during a panic attack, so that the individual becomes reluctant to be alone or in public places away from home. When many situations of the kind are avoided the diagnosis of Agoraphobia with Panic Attacks should be made (p. 226) rather than Panic Disorder.

Associated features. The individual often develops varying degrees of nervousness and apprehension between attacks. This nervousness and apprehension is characterized by the usual manifestations of apprehensive expectation, vigilance and scanning, motor tension, and autonomic hyperactivity.

Age at onset. The disorder often begins in late adolescence or early adult life, but may occur initially in mid-adult life.

Course. The disorder may be limited to a single brief period lasting several weeks or months, recur several times, or become chronic.

Impairment. Except when the disorder is severe or complicated by Agoraphobia, it is rarely incapacitating.

Complications. The complication of Agoraphobia with Panic Attacks has been mentioned above. Other complications include abuse of alcohol and antianxiety medications, and Depressive Disorders.

Predisposing factors. Separation Anxiety Disorder in childhood and sudden object loss apparently predispose to the development of this disorder.

Prevalence. The disorder is apparently common.

Sex ratio. This condition is diagnosed much more commonly in women.

Differential diagnosis. **Physical disorders** such as **hypoglycemia, pheochromocytoma,** and **hyperthyroidism,** all of which can cause similar symptoms, must be ruled out.

In **Withdrawal** from some substances, such as **barbiturates,** and in some **Substance Intoxications,** such as due to **caffeine** or **amphetamines,** there may be panic attacks. Panic Disorder should not be diagnosed when the panic attacks are due to Substance-induced Organic Mental Disorder.

In **Schizophrenia, Major Depression,** or **Somatization Disorder** panic attacks may occur. However, the diagnosis of Panic Disorder is not made if the panic attacks are due to these other disorders.

Generalized Anxiety Disorder may be confused with the chronic anxiety that often develops between panic attacks in Panic Disorder. A history of recurrent panic attacks precludes Generalized Anxiety Disorder.

In **Simple** or **Social Phobia,** the individual may develop panic attacks if exposed to the phobic stimulus. However, in Panic Disorder, the individual is never certain which situations provoke panic attacks.

Diagnostic criteria for Panic Disorder

A. At least three panic attacks within a three-week period in circumstances other than during marked physical exertion or in a life-threatening situation. The attacks are not precipitated only by exposure to a circumscribed phobic stimulus.

B. Panic attacks are manifested by discrete periods of apprehension **or** fear, and at least four of the following symptoms appear during each attack:

    (1) dyspnea
    (2) palpitations
    (3) chest pain or discomfort
    (4) choking or smothering sensations
    (5) dizziness, vertigo, or unsteady feelings
    (6) feelings of unreality
    (7) paresthesias (tingling in hands or feet)
    (8) hot and cold flashes
    (9) sweating
    (10) faintness
    (11) trembling or shaking

(12) fear of dying, going crazy, or doing something uncontrolled during an attack

C. Not due to a physical disorder or another mental disorder, such as Major Depression, Somatization Disorder, or Schizophrenia.

D. The disorder is not associated with Agoraphobia (p. 227).

300.02   Generalized Anxiety Disorder

The essential feature is generalized, persistent anxiety of at least one month's duration without the specific symptoms that characterize Phobic Disorders (phobias), Panic Disorder (panic attacks), or Obsessive Compulsive Disorder (obsessions or compulsions). The diagnosis is not made if the disturbance is due to another physical or mental disorder, such as hyperthyroidism or Major Depression.

Although the specific manifestations of the anxiety vary from individual to individual, generally there are signs of motor tension, autonomic hyperactivity, apprehensive expectation, and vigilance and scanning.

(1) *Motor tension.* Shakiness, jitteriness, jumpiness, trembling, tension, muscle aches, fatigability, and inability to relax are common complaints. There may also be eyelid twitch, furrowed brow, strained face, fidgeting, restlessness, easy startle, and sighing respiration.

(2) *Autonomic hyperactivity.* There may be sweating, heart pounding or racing, cold, clammy hands, dry mouth, dizziness, light-headedness, paresthesias (tingling in hands or feet), upset stomach, hot or cold spells, frequent urination, diarrhea, discomfort in the pit of the stomach, lump in the throat, flushing, pallor, and high resting pulse and respiration rate.

(3) *Apprehensive expectation.* The individual is generally apprehensive and continually feels anxious, worries, ruminates, and anticipates that something bad will happen to himself or herself (e.g., fear of fainting, losing control, dying) or to others (e.g., family members may become ill or injured in an accident).

(4) *Vigilance and scanning.* Apprehensive expectation may cause hyper-attentiveness so that the individual feels "on edge," impatient, or irritable. There may be complaints of distractibility, difficulty in concentrating, insomnia, difficulty in falling asleep, interrupted sleep, and fatigue on awakening.

Associated features. Mild depressive symptoms are common.

Impairment. Impairment in social or occupational functioning is rarely more than mild.

Complications. Abuse of alcohol, barbiturates, and antianxiety medications is common.

Age at onset, course, predisposing factors, prevalence, sex ratio, and familial pattern. No information.

Differential diagnosis. Physical disorders, such as hyperthyroidism, and Organic Mental Disorders, such as Caffeine Intoxication, must be ruled out.

In Adjustment Disorder with Anxious Mood, the full symptom picture required to meet the criteria for Generalized Anxiety Disorder is generally not present, the duration of the disturbance is usually less than a month, and a psychosocial stressor must be recognized.

In Schizophrenia, Depressive Disorders, Hypochondriasis, Obsessive Compulsive Disorder, and many other mental disorders, generalized and persistent anxiety is often a prominent symptom. The diagnosis of Generalized Anxiety Disorder is not made if the anxiety is judged to be due to another mental disorder.

In Panic Disorder there is often severe chronic anxiety between panic attacks. If the panic attacks are overlooked, an incorrect diagnosis of Generalized Anxiety Disorder may be made.

Diagnostic criteria for Generalized Anxiety Disorder

A. Generalized, persistent anxiety is manifested by symptoms from three of the following four categories:

(1) *motor tension*: shakiness, jitteriness, jumpiness, trembling, tension, muscle aches, fatigability, inability to relax, eyelid twitch, furrowed brow, strained face, fidgeting, restlessness, easy startle

(2) *autonomic hyperactivity*: sweating, heart pounding or racing, cold, clammy hands, dry mouth, dizziness, light-headedness, paresthesias (tingling in hands or feet), upset stomach, hot or cold spells, frequent urination, diarrhea, discomfort in the pit of the stomach, lump in the throat, flushing, pallor, high resting pulse and respiration rate

(3) *apprehensive expectation*: anxiety, worry, fear, rumination, and anticipation of misfortune to self or others

(4) *vigilance and scanning*: hyperattentiveness resulting in distractibility, difficulty in concentrating, insomnia, feeling "on edge," irritability, impatience

B. The anxious mood has been continuous for at least one month.

C. Not due to another mental disorder, such as a Depressive Disorder or Schizophrenia.

D. At least 18 years of age.

300.30   Obsessive Compulsive Disorder (or Obsessive Compulsive Neurosis)
The essential features are recurrent obsessions or compulsions. *Obsessions* are recurrent, persistent ideas, thoughts, images, or impulses that are ego-dystonic, that is, they are not experienced as voluntarily produced, but rather as thoughts that invade consciousness and are experienced as senseless or repugnant. Attempts are made to ignore or suppress them. *Compulsions* are repetitive and seemingly purposeful behaviors that are performed according to certain rules or in a stereotyped fashion. The behavior is not an end in itself, but is designed to produce or to prevent some future event or situation. However, the activity is not connected in a realistic way with what it is designed to produce or prevent, or may be clearly excessive. The act is performed with a sense of subjective compulsion coupled with a desire to resist the compulsion (at least initially). The individual generally recognizes the senselessness of the behavior (this may not be true for young children) and does not derive pleasure from carrying out the activity, although it provides a release of tension.

The most common obsessions are repetitive thoughts of violence (e.g., killing one's child), contamination (e.g., becoming infected by shaking hands), and doubt (e.g., repeatedly wondering whether one has performed some action, such as having hurt someone in a traffic accident). The most common compulsions involve hand-washing, counting, checking, and touching.

When the individual attempts to resist a compulsion, there is a sense of mounting tension that can be immediately relieved by yielding to the compulsion. In the course of the illness, after repeated failure at resisting the compulsions, the individual may give in to them and no longer experience a desire to resist them.

Associated features. Depression and anxiety are common. Frequently there is phobic avoidance of situations that involve the content of the obsessions, such as dirt or contamination.

Age at onset. Although the disorder usually begins in adolescence or early adulthood, it may begin in childhood.

Course. The course is usually chronic, with waxing and waning of symptoms.

Impairment. Impairment is generally moderate to severe. In some cases compulsions may become the major life activity.

Complications. Complications include Major Depression and the abuse of alcohol and antianxiety medications.

Predisposing factors. No information.

Prevalence. The disorder is apparently rare in the general population.

Sex ratio. This disorder is equally common in males and in females.

Differential diagnosis. Some activities, such as **eating, sexual behavior (e.g., Paraphilias), gambling, or drinking, when engaged in excessively** may be referred to as "compulsive". However, these activities are not true compulsions, because the individual derives pleasure from the particular activity and may wish to resist it only because of its secondary deleterious consequences.

Obsessive brooding, rumination or **preoccupation,** i.e., excessive and repetitive thinking about real or potentially unpleasant circumstances, or indecisive consideration of alternatives lacks the quality of being ego-dystonic, because the individual generally regards the ideation as meaningful, although possibly excessive. Therefore, these are not true obsessions.

In **Schizophrenia,** stereotyped behavior is common, but can be explained by delusions rather than as being ego-dystonic. Obsessions and compulsions sometimes occur transiently during the prodromal phase of Schizophrenia. In such cases the diagnosis of Obsessive Compulsive Disorder is not made. **Tourette's Disorder, Schizophrenia, Major Depression** and, very rarely, **Organic Mental Disorder** may have obsessions and compulsions as symptoms, but in such instances the diagnosis Obsessive Compulsive Disorder is not made. However, Obsessive Compulsive Disorder may precede the development of a Major Depression, in which case both diagnoses should be recorded.

Diagnostic criteria for Obsessive Compulsive Disorder

A. Either obsessions or compulsions:

Obsessions: recurrent, persistent ideas, thoughts, images, or impulses that are ego-dystonic, i.e., they are not experienced as voluntarily produced, but rather as thoughts that invade consciousness and are experienced as senseless or repugnant. Attempts are made to ignore or suppress them.

Compulsions: repetitive and seemingly purposeful behaviors that are performed according to certain rules or in a stereotyped fashion. The behavior is not an end in itself, but is designed to produce or prevent some future event or situation. However, either the activity is not connected in a realistic way with what it is designed to produce or prevent, or may be clearly excessive. The act is performed with a sense of subjective compulsion coupled with a desire to resist the compulsion (at least initially). The individual generally recognizes the senselessness of the behavior (this may not be true for young children) and does not derive pleasure from carrying out the activity, although it provides a release of tension.

B. The obsessions or compulsions are a significant source of distress to the individual or interfere with social or role functioning.

C. Not due to another mental disorder, such as Tourette's Disorder, Schizophrenia, Major Depression, or Organic Mental Disorder.

308.30   Post-traumatic Stress Disorder, Acute

309.81   Post-traumatic Stress Disorder, Chronic or Delayed

The essential feature is the development of characteristic symptoms following a psychologically traumatic event that is generally outside the range of usual human experience.

The characteristic symptoms involve reexperiencing the traumatic event; numbing of responsiveness to, or reduced involvement with, the external world; and a variety of autonomic, dysphoric, or cognitive symptoms.

The stressor producing this syndrome would evoke significant symptoms of distress in most people, and is generally outside the range of such common experiences as simple bereavement, chronic illness, business losses, or marital conflict. The trauma may be experienced alone (rape or assault) or in the company of groups of people (military combat). Stressors producing this disorder include natural disasters (floods, earthquakes), accidental man-made disasters (car accidents with serious physical injury, airplane crashes, large fires), or deliberate man-made disasters (bombing, torture, death camps). Some stressors frequently produce the disorder (e.g., torture) and others produce it only occasionally (e.g., car accidents). Frequently there is a concomitant physical component to the trauma which may even involve direct damage to the central nervous system (e.g., malnutrition, head trauma). The disorder is apparently more severe and longer lasting when the stressor is of human design. The severity of the stressor should be recorded and the specific stressor may be noted on Axis IV (p. 26).

The traumatic event can be reexperienced in a variety of ways. Commonly the individual has recurrent painful, intrusive recollections of the event or recurrent dreams or nightmares during which the event is reexperienced. In rare instances there are dissociativelike states, lasting from a few minutes to several hours or even days, during which components of the event are relived and the individual behaves as though experiencing the event at that moment. Such states have been reported in combat veterans. Diminished responsiveness to the external world, referred to as "psychic numbing" or "emotional anesthesia," usually begins soon after the traumatic event. A person may complain of feeling detached or estranged from other people, that he or she has lost the ability to become interested in previously enjoyed significant activities, or that the ability to feel emotions of any type, especially those associated with intimacy, tenderness, and sexuality, is markedly decreased.

After experiencing the stressor, many develop symptoms of excessive autonomic arousal, such as hyperalertness, exaggerated startle response, and difficulty falling asleep. Recurrent nightmares during which the traumatic event is relived and which are sometimes accompanied by middle or terminal sleep disturbance may be present. Some complain of impaired memory or difficulty in concentrating or completing tasks. In the case of a life-threatening trauma shared with others, survivors often describe painful guilt feelings about surviving when many did not, or about the things they had to do in order to survive. Activities or situations that may arouse recollections of the traumatic event are often avoided. Symptoms characteristic of Post-traumatic Stress Disorder are often intensified when the individual is exposed to situations or activities that resemble or symbolize the original trauma (e.g., cold snowy weather or uniformed guards for death-camp survivors, hot, humid weather for veterans of the South Pacific).

Associated features. Symptoms of depression and anxiety are common, and in some instances may be sufficiently severe to be diagnosed as an Anxiety or Depressive Disorder. Increased irritability may be associated with sporadic and unpredictable explosions of aggressive behavior, upon even minimal or no provocation. The latter symptom has been reported to be particularly characteristic of war veterans with this disorder. Impulsive behavior can occur, such as sudden trips, unexplained absences, or changes in life-style or residence. Survivors of death camps sometimes have symptoms of an Organic Mental Disorder, such as failing memory, difficulty in concentrating, emotional lability, autonomic lability, headache, and vertigo.

Age at onset. The disorder can occur at any age, including during childhood.

Course and subtypes. Symptoms may begin immediately or soon after the trauma. It is not unusual, however, for the symptoms to emerge after a latency period of months or years following the trauma.

When the symptoms begin within six months of the trauma and have not lasted more than six months, the acute subtype is diagnosed, and the prognosis for remission is good. If the symptoms either develop more than six months after the trauma or last six months or more, the chronic or delayed subtype is diagnosed.

Impairment and complications. Impairment may either be mild or affect nearly every aspect of life. Phobic avoidance of situations or activities resembling or symbolizing the original trauma may result in occupational or recreational impairment. "Psychic numbing" may interfere with interpersonal relationships, such as marriage or family life. Emotional lability, depression, and guilt may result in self-defeating behavior or suicidal actions. Substance Use Disorders may develop.

Predisposing factors. Preexisting psychopathology apparently predisposes to the development of the disorder.

Prevalence. No information.

Sex ratio and familial pattern. No information.

Differential diagnosis. If an **Anxiety, Depressive,** or **Organic Mental Disorder** develops following the trauma, these diagnoses should also be made.

In **Adjustment Disorder,** the stressor is usually less severe and within the range of common experience; and the characteristic symptoms of Post-traumatic Stress Disorder, such as reexperiencing the trauma, are absent.

Diagnostic criteria for Post-traumatic Stress Disorder

A. Existence of a recognizable stressor that would evoke significant symptoms of distress in almost everyone.

B. Reexperiencing of the trauma as evidenced by at least one of the following:

(1) recurrent and intrusive recollections of the event
(2) recurrent dreams of the event
(3) sudden acting or feeling as if the traumatic event were reoccurring, because of an association with an environmental or ideational stimulus

C. Numbing of responsiveness to or reduced involvement with the external world, beginning some time after the trauma, as shown by at least one of the following:

(1) markedly diminished interest in one or more significant activities
(2) feeling of detachment or estrangement from others
(3) constricted affect

D. At least two of the following symptoms that were not present before the trauma:

(1) hyperalertness or exaggerated startle response
(2) sleep disturbance
(3) guilt about surviving when others have not, or about behavior required for survival
(4) memory impairment or trouble concentrating
(5) avoidance of activities that arouse recollection of the traumatic event
(6) intensification of symptoms by exposure to events that symbolize or resemble the traumatic event

SUBTYPES

Post-traumatic Stress Disorder, Acute

A. Onset of symptoms within six months of the trauma.

B. Duration of symptoms less than six months.

Post-traumatic Stress Disorder, Chronic or Delayed

Either of the following, or both:

(1) duration of symptoms six months or more (chronic)
(2) onset of symptoms at least six months after the trauma (delayed)

300.00   Atypical Anxiety Disorder
This category should be used when the individual appears to have an Anxiety Disorder that does not meet the criteria for any of the above specified conditions.

Index

All page numbers in **bold** type refer to tables or figures in the text.